To Milo

Contents

I

introduction

The teen years are that particular period in life when ideals are formed and important goals set. A time when a person can be drawn into an exciting world where work and play are balanced. It can also be the time when a youth takes a negative path. It is certainly a time when help is needed. So often parents, because of their close contact and because of their roles as disciplinarians, are handicapped by past misunderstandings. Ministers and teachers are in a better position to help the teenager and certainly will want to. It should be fun for both the helped and the helper.

This book, *Breaking Communication Barriers with Roleplay,* is a guide for ministers or teachers who want some effective tools to reach the teenage members of their congregation or classes. If you are searching for such tools, this is the book for you.

If a picture is worth a thousand words, then how much more should an actual experience be worth! You can talk to someone until your voice becomes hoarse and see clearly you are not getting anywhere. It's discouraging and frustrating! A far more effective technique is to put your person into a roleplay situation—and pit him against an antagonist! The situation soon becomes real to him and he will have to find realistic answers. The answers a player is forced to come up with are his own and will mean a great deal more to him. The situation can then be further discussed as being a universal problem. When the player understands that this is also his own particular problem, he will continue to search on his own.

Roleplaying sometimes even has advantages over one-to-one counseling. Not only is one-to-one counseling time consuming, but very often the need for it does not present itself. A teen will not usually ask a minister or teacher for help even in serious problems, much less for simple communication difficulties. He is sometimes unaware of the need for help. If parents bring attention to a youth by pointing out the problem, he may be sullen and unreceptive. It may be hard for him to level and bring out his true feelings and emotions on any subject.

In roleplaying, on the other hand, the teenager is only playing a part in a drama. Because it is not a threatening situation, a young boy or girl can try out different ways of reacting and can be more open about real feelings. With two casts, he or she can watch how someone else plays the same part and notice the reaction it gets. Later a player may want to try a new way of reacting in the same role or a similar one.

In all counseling a minister or teacher must be very careful to avoid sounding judgmental or as if he or she is preaching. All help must be subtle and have a light touch. This is not always easy. Giving help is much easier and more effective in a roleplaying situation because the teenager himself is in a position to see the wisdom of the remark in relation to the role action.

Even rap sessions among peers do not always allow teenagers the freedom to communicate. Talking is too often done by the glib speaker and the more confident youth, not by those most needing the help. This can be remedied by giving youths a role to play. All will feel more secure with a problem to work out and a definite goal. No one will be left on the fringes feeling lonely and unwanted. In the role as observer, the conductor is in a unique position to see where help is needed and, as part of the method of roleplaying, is able to point this out in a non-condemning way.

The teen years are a sensitive age when small hurts become magnified and tend to drive youths in the wrong direction. But while the teen is playing an impersonal role, many things can be brought out without touching or damaging his sensitive ego. Often a youth does not realize why some of his actions, or his words, or ways of expressing himself get negative reactions—not only from his elders but his peers as well. He feels he is being picked on and even that everyone is being deliberately mean. In roleplaying he may get a more objective view.

To illustrate what I mean let me describe what happened one roleplaying weekend because of a simple dialoguing quirk: Two boys were almost at the point of physical blows when one of them shouted, "You haven't answered my question!" To which the other answered, "Hey, man, you don't ask a question. A question expects an honest answer. Your questions expect your *own* answers!"

This boy had been unaware that he always expected his own particular answer to questions. The rest of the group helped him to see how his habit was irritating friends and foes alike. Very often quirks of this type (and other snags that interfere with a free exchange of ideas) can be brought out in a frank discussion following the playing of the role.

"So roleplaying's nothing new," you may say, "I do it all the time." Even if you do I would like to encourage you to try this method and these roles. As the conductor, your position is something like that of a football coach who sends his player out into the field with a pep talk. You support each player in his role while stimulating a frank conflict between players.

Roleplaying, as set forth in this book, helps you to dig out problems caused by the lack of listening and understanding. It can bring to the surface frustrations, guilts, and resentments. Roles are structured to help with the numerous problems of teenagers, all the way from how to give (or not to give!) advice and take criticism to how to give and accept love. Although help is given with each stage of the roleplay, the roles allow for and encourage the reader's own creativeness.

In facing today's world, the three "L's" of Listening, Leveling, and Loving are as important as the three "R's" of Reading, 'Riting, and 'Rithmetic. The need for the first two of these "L's," sensitive listening and leveling, is made drastically clear in roleplaying, for without them a roleplay will not move forward. Loving, the third "L," is important because the world the teenager aims for should be a world peopled with intimate friends who care, not just a world of mere acquaintances. Courtship relationships are brought out in a number of roles, from "puppy love" to manipulating someone into marriage.

Games are used to focus some of the main points brought out in the roleplaying. These games are a unique and useful feature because they provide the teenager with understanding and with a new way to react. The games "Mimic Charades" and "I-Thou Feedback," for example, teach listening techniques. Another game, "Manipulative Basketball," has players use exaggeration to understand and thus overcome manipulation. (Manipulating is using a non-leveling approach in relationships, which tends to be self-defeating.) The "Who Is Me?" and "PAC Pinball" games start a youth out on the adventure of discovering himself. The Symbol Game helps him become aware of his potentialities while encouraging him to set goals and become involved in something he is "turned on" by. One game helps youths give "Fuzzies" (compliments) rather than "pricklies" (put-downs). Another gives one player a chance to show love in adverse circumstances while allowing another player a chance to release pent-up resentment.

The roles in this book are simple and designed especially for the beginning roleplaying conductor—one who may, or may not, have had some counseling experience. A psychoanalyst or experienced therapist (who has the know-how to deal with difficult problems if they arise) can easily change or deepen these roles

9

to deal with more traumatic experiences. The book is not addressed to the psychiatrists or psychologists who are usually working with the abnormal on a one-to-one basis, for the roles try merely to deal with the communicating difficulties of normal youth.

A beginning conductor (that is, the director of the roleplay) will find it helpful to read over all of the instructions in chapter 2 and some of the suggestions with the roles before starting to roleplay. Some of this material, particularly in chapter 2, may seem quite technical to a newcomer. However, this book deals with many ways to get the most out of roleplaying, so don't be concerned to learn every technique or concept at once. After you have tried conducting for a while, refer back to chapter 2 for new ideas to try.

Conducting roleplays does not require any special wisdom or professional training; the skills you need are mainly those of listening and observing. As you become more proficient in this role of observer, you will be able to detect when one player is manipulating another or where the "child" in the youth has gained the upper hand. At first it would be well just to concentrate on giving your players the information they will need. You could start out just by reading the information to them (being careful to leave out material not meant to be given); but you will get much better results if you talk directly to your players, in a personal tone and using your own words.

Teenagers today are on the threshold of a dramatically changing world and need all the help they can get before being thrust into it. This book provides tools for you to help them. Dare you pass up the chance?

2

instructions

General Information

A roleplay, like an ordinary play, has a situation with a conflict. In roleplaying, however, a potential conflict is assigned to each of the players in a given situation, but they must supply their own dialogue and attempt their own solution. The solution in itself is not a primary aim in roleplaying. What is important is learning more effective methods of handling problems. In this book most of the roleplays concentrate on how the players handle the situation rather than on the issue itself.

You will have no need for scenery or props. A small room, preferably carpeted, will create the right atmosphere. Enough chairs should be supplied for all to sit comfortably around a center area that is used for the stage. Any person with authority can direct the roleplays in this book. Although the term "facilitator" is used in therapeutic roleplay, here the director will simply be known as the "conductor."

The conductor must remember that the main purpose is to help the role-players and audience gain new understanding. Roleplaying is an inductive method of learning and the insight is gained either during or after the playing. Keep in mind that in roleplaying the person usually acts, thinks, and feels as he does in real life, but he is not under pressure so he can operate in a condition devoid of threat. It is because of this that the defects which cripple communication can be dealt with in a gentle way.

Roleplaying is a living, changing instrument and each little difference may be pointing out some important fact. Hurts, frustrations, and the emotions of anger and resentment should be watched for during the roleplay. Bad listening or speaking habits and irritating quirks of expression may be observed and helped during discussions. The way facts are presented should be noted and dealt with in a constructive way.

Emotion can be released in roleplaying. Teenagers often have a desperate need to rid themselves of feelings held in. In roleplaying they can do this in a fairly impersonal way. Most families cannot afford a psychiatrist just for dialoguing disabilities. Nor can they bring themselves to bother a minister or teacher for what might seem just minor trouble. Yet a little patience may ease hurt or tension, and may even head a youth off from the path towards serious crises such as violence or suicide.

A few general methods used in therapeutic roleplay can help point out snags in our dialoguing abilities. One method, which helps both the players and the audience to understand what is happening, is to stop the roleplay and ask the players how they are feeling.[1] Various answers are given, such as: frustrated, hurt, angry, puzzled, etc. These are often an indication of some dialoguing difficulty.

There are several ways to go about explaining such feelings:

a. If you are a beginning conductor you will probably feel more comfortable having a *discussion* about why players feel as they do, and how the dialogue could be handled in a better way. You may want to try the roleplay with two casts and then discuss why one player was getting himself and his ideas across better than another. Guide the players by your own insight into the situation.

b. If you are a more experienced conductor or someone who has used some counseling techniques, you might try a different method, namely "modeling." In simple language, this just means providing a model for your players to follow. If you can understand why a player is unable to get his ideas across, or why he is antagonizing the other players, or even why he is losing out in the conflict, you can get your idea over better by showing him rather than just telling him. The audience can also learn by this.

Basic Instructions:

1. Roles should not be attempted without someone in authority conducting them. This is especially important with teenagers. It is also advisable to forbid anyone to be a part of the audience who is not willing to take part in the roleplaying. This is to prevent a non-participating audience from making fun of the players.

2. In selecting a first role, a beginning conductor is advised not to try the

12

personification roles or roles without conflict for they are harder to conduct and harder to play. A role with a strong conflict and players who have a great deal of self-confidence are easier to conduct.

3. The conductor need not be concerned that teenagers are playing the parts of parents, grandparents, or small children. Roleplaying seems to have some magic of its own that surpasses even other drama. Once fully in the role, a person will play it for real: a teenage girl will suddenly *become* a grandmother or an eight-year-old sister.

4. To make roleplaying more effective, the conductor should describe the role to each player, individually, in front of the audience. The other characters should be out of the room so that they will only be aware of their own situations. (In the case of two casts, the two people with the same role should be briefed together. Also, the second cast should be out of the room when the first cast performs.)

5. The players will find it easier to use the actual first name of their co-players in the roleplay rather than the one given in the role. The conductor can use the terms "girl-part" or "Basil-part" or something like "father," "grandmother," when he is giving his instructions, to help with this style of identification. If it seems difficult at first, the conductor should be guided by what seems comfortable.

6. In giving instructions, the conductor should try to be in sympathy with the player he is addressing, and also with the instructions he is giving. He should have a heart-to-heart talk with the player, giving him the facts, but not telling him how to use them or what to say. The conductor will be trying to intensify or heighten the conflict, and psychologically trying to encourage the player and put him in the mood of the role. If the conductor himself can get in the mood of the role, he may then subconsciously give it to the player.

Except in a few specified instances (see instructions for some of the games), the conductor should give the directions from this book *in his own words*, personalizing them by using the second person. With this personal touch, his sympathy for a role and for the person playing it will come across to all his players.

7. The role-dialogue is not meant to be given to the players. The aim is to allow the players to project their own personalities into the roles and nothing should hinder this. The role-dialogue given with each role isn't meant to be real dialogue but is given simply to show the conductor different points that will be helpful. Some of the dialogue is stiff and unreal, because I have concentrated on points rather than realism. At various times it will indicate: the type of player needed for the role, the aim of the roleplay, how leveling brings the conflict into the open and accelerates the action, how put-downs, sarcasm, and general nastiness slow the action, and how words indicate whether the parent, adult, or child is predominating in the player.

8. The conductor should be careful to set the scene so that each player is

plunged into the role and can feel a part of it. The opening scenes given are simply one way the roles can be started. If some other scene has more meaning for your particular youths, by all means use it instead.

9. The players can bring in additional complications along the lines of those in the role. They should always feel free to pursue complications that have more meaning for them. (Sometimes the problems that youths find hard to express surface in this way.)

10. Remember, there is no set way that a role has to be played. Each time it will differ because the people involved are different. Changing just one player could make a whole new ball game. In other words *do not force a solution.* No one should be made to feel that he is being pushed into a mold. The solution must come from the players or from a suggestive "modeling" by the conductor. It should aim at being a no-win, no-lose compromise. Sometimes it may just come to a draw where one or the other of the players is only willing to think it over. Remember, *how* the player reaches the solution (or aims towards it) is the important thing.

11. The conductor can give out information which one person is withholding, and he can add more information which would help bring about a solution. This can be accomplished by a faked phone call, or by sending in another player with specific instructions. A note can be used when only one player should have the added information. Most technical problems can be solved by giving new information in the same way.

12. A time-shift can be used if it will help in solving a problem or reaching a solution. The conductor simply says something like: "It is now the evening of the next day, and . . . ."

13. Sometimes a player is using the role only as an emotional release and his mind is not set on problem solving. The youth may need to rid himself of some suppressed feelings so this should be allowed to continue for a short time. However, it should not be allowed to continue long enough to bore the rest of the cast and the audience. The conductor should call "cut" and use his own judgment in dealing with it. A simple way is to mention that the roleplay has gotten away from the problem and suggest that the players get back to the issues of the role.

14. A question a new conductor might ask is: When do I stop the roleplaying? Most conductors quickly learn when to stop, but if you are just beginning, a good rule to follow is to watch for the interest of the players and the audience. Some roleplays may be long and drawn out. When something constructive is taking place, however, it will be dramatically interesting even through minutes of silence. If a conductor is in doubt, he should simply stop the playing, get the reaction of the players up to that point, and ask them if they would like to continue. Sometimes the roleplayers are having a great time and would continue indefinitely. The audience should then have some say in its continuance. When a compromise or a solution is reached the roleplaying should

be stopped. Usually when problem solving is not taking place (and it seems impossible to achieve it) the roleplaying should be discontinued.

15. After the roleplaying, be sure to allow the players to give their reactions before opening up discussion to the audience.

Selection of Players:

Players will sometimes choose their roles voluntarily. This in itself can bring out a number of interesting insights. However, a great deal more can be accomplished if the conductor puts players into roles where he can see they will be helped. It stands to reason that the better the conductor knows his players (and the more sensitive he is to their needs) the more effective the roleplaying will be.

In selecting players for most roles, you will probably want them evenly matched, or as close to this as you can come.

a. The first exception to this would be when there is no conflict, so that the abilities of the players are not important.

b. The second exception would be where identification with the role is more important than the ability of the player.

c. A third exception would be for a new conductor starting out. Two extremely shy youths might be evenly matched, but in a role without a conflict neither might want to take the initiative, making an inexperienced conductor at least uneasy.

d. The fourth exception would be certain roles that are designed to point out the comparative abilities of the players, and players should be selected for them accordingly. In this book, a person with a strong personality will be designated as a *heavyweight* in contrast to the shy person designated as a *lightweight*. [2] Roleplays that require heavyweights and lightweights in opposition are ones like "Unwarranted Help" (p. 27) and "Did It Have to Be Divorce?" (p. 114).

These ability roles are given for a twofold purpose:

First, the conductor should be trying to show a person who has strong opinions (and the confidence to back them up) that sometimes he may have to tone them down, so that another person who does not come on as strong can be allowed the freedom to express himself and respond. It might help to point out to the heavyweight player that to win is not the only consideration in interpersonal relations, and that other players have needs that he ought to be aware of. The authors of *The Intimate Enemy* suggest that heavyweights should, figuratively speaking, hold one arm behind their backs when engaging a lightweight player.

Second, the conductor should be trying to help a lightweight player speak up for his rights. If possible an attempt should be made to show the lightweight player why he is failing to gain his points. Respect for oneself and for one's rights is a quality everyone should have, and it should be worth fighting for. Leveling about these feelings is a first step to winning. In *The Intimate Enemy,*

Bach and Wyden use the lack of leveling to head the list of drawbacks to the success of their methods.[3]

e. A fifth exception would be similar to the one above, but where a certain situation is needed and a player with more fighting ability would push harder; for example: "Broken Plans for Marriage" (p. 109).

What to Watch for and Bring Up During the Discussion:

1. A major stumbling block to any dialogue is lack of leveling. The same applies in roleplaying. When players hold back their own feelings, or the facts they have been given, the roleplay becomes bogged down with nothing moving. The conductor should call "cut" and ask the players how they are feeling. Various answers—from feeling frustrated to feeling confused—will indicate the plight of the players. The conductor could then "model." He simply steps in and plays one of the roles—telling the truth in a simple, but gentle and loving way. It gets amazing results!

2. Sometimes, during a crisis or immediately afterwards while the situation is still sensitive, someone will start preaching or giving advice. If this happens during a roleplay, point out that this tends to antagonize instead of resolving difficulties. Preaching, advice, and judgmental suggestions almost always alienate people. In roleplaying it may provoke a sharp retort. Thomas Gordon, in his book *Parent Effectiveness Training* (hereafter called *P.E.T.*), has listed preachiness among the responses he advises people not to make if they want to engage in "Active Listening." These are listed in this book with the game, "I-Thou Feedback" at the end of chapter 3 (p. 39).

3. Like a remedial teacher, you should look for weaknesses in the way a player presents his facts. A player who has a poor opinion of himself may be defeated before he even starts. Watch for the player who presents his facts in a halfhearted way as if he did not expect to win. You might use some modeling here to advantage. Present the facts with firmness and conviction and demonstrate the difference it makes on those who are listening.

4. Each player should have the freedom to make his own decisions. Watch for places where this is being interfered with. This does not mean, however, that players who are taking the parts of someone in a position of authority cannot warn others of the dangers or consequences of their decisions.

5. Watch for the places where a player is not listening carefully enough. He may be so wrapped up in his own view that the other player is not coming through to him. This hinders the solving of the conflict. Watch also for the player who is so emotionally involved or is so impatient that he is closing off his listening capactiy.

6. Watch for parts of the instruction which a player forgets. There is usually a reason for forgetting, and it may be important. Ask the player if he wants to take a closer look at why he forgot. (In a few roles ignoring facts may be

prudent; for example: "Forces Crippling the Ego" [p. 77].)

7. Also, watch for the times when players distort or block out information. The player may have a strong opinion, prejudice, or bias, and this may influence how he hears and deals with the facts.

8. Watch for "body language." Tone of voice, gestures and other body movements, expressions on the face, and just the way a word is spoken can sometimes take on more importance than the word itself. A player's demeanor may be unconsciously shouting something completely opposed to his words. Even a word like "oaf" can be a term of endearment if handled in a certain way.

Very often, youths are unaware of how they are coming across. Though sometimes in roleplaying the players can understand their effect on others by the results they get, there are other times when they are completely unaware of what caused such a reaction. The conductor should jot down these times during the playing of the role. Then, during the discussion, he can jog the memory of the players by bringing up the instances of the subconscious tone of voice and the reaction it received.

9. Sometimes it is better to let two people work out a conflict alone without a third party's interference. If someone does interfere but not in a way that significantly disrupts the playing, let it go on and point it out later in the discussion following the roleplay. (Disruptions are sometimes inserted as part of the role by using a prop player—one with definite instructions to follow until the scene becomes emotionally difficult. This should be brought out in the discussion period so all are aware of the reason for the disruptions.)

10. Occasionally one player may be hindering the dialogue and may have to be dealt with before the action can go forward. It is important that he be dealt with in a way that helps rather than antagonizes him. The roleplay can be stopped and the players asked how they are feeling. This may bring out the reason for the offending player's actions or it may bring out the other players' reaction to a dialoguing quirk. If, in a roleplay with three characters, it is established that antagonism between two of them prevents them from dealing with the third (as in RP 10, p. 83), the third player may be advised to deal with each of these antagonists individually.

11. Watch for parallel speaking. Players who are talking about the same subject but are developing their own cases so independently that they do not intersect. In other words, neither party is listening to his opponent.

12. We can think much faster than a speaker can talk.[4] How are the players using this extra listening time? They can use it to best advantage if they analyze their opponent's points and the direction he seems to be going. They should, however, listen not merely to his intellectual points but also to the direction of his feelings.

13. Salesmanship is great for selling but not always for solving interpersonal relations. Watch for the person coming on too strong or using propaganda tricks.

Nichols and Stevens, in their book *Are You Listening?*, list seven propaganda tricks that salesmen use.[5] Here are some ways these tricks crop up in roleplaying:

a. *Name calling*—using labels that produce emotion, usually with an implied threat. A roleplayer could say: "Your point is distasteful to anyone of intelligence." "You sound like a Communist."

b. *Glowing terms*—glittering generalities that put our own cause in a favorable light. Example (taken from "Broken Plans for Marriage" RP 14, p. 109): "Traveling with the Ballet all over the world will make a full and exciting life which I'm sure you wouldn't want to miss. We'll never lack for money. Friends, hobbies, fame—we'll have a wonderful time together."

c. *"Authorities say"*—making our cause respectable by association. Example: "I know you have a lot of respect for science and this is what scientists have found."

d. *Testimonials*—using respect for well-known people to promote our own point. A roleplayer could say: "Lincoln used this point and what's good enough for old Abe is good enough for me!"

e. *Editing*—card stacking material to promote our own cause, neglecting to mention the other side. Example (taken from RP 6, p. 49): "Constance honey, this income property leaves me no time for my inventing. There's always a drippy faucet, or a door lock that needs fixing, or a tenant who's lost his keys, or . . . ."

f. *Using Trust*—playing on people's trust of those like themselves and their distrust of others. A roleplayer could say: "I know you can understand my point—we're both men and we know how a man feels when he gets upstaged by a woman."

g. *Bandwagon*—playing on follow-the-crowd instincts. Example (from RP 5, p. 46): "Gosh, Lee, everyone will be there. Do you want them to think you weren't invited?"

14. Watch for *I-Messages* and *You-Messages*.[6]

You-Messages tend to be a put-down and do not help a relationship. Examples: "Will you stop that? You're acting like a child!" "You're old enough to know better than that!" "You're so messy and disorganized! Why can't you do things right for once?"

I-Messages are a form of leveling, telling how *you* feel about a situation rather than what you feel someone else should or should not be doing. This type of message is more acceptable to another person. Example: "I'm discouraged when I walk in and see this mess. A hang-up of mine is trying to get a meal in a dirty kitchen."

A teenager to a younger sister, instead of saying, "You're a stinking little pest, and you bug me!" might try, this: "Susy, I'm upset! I'm trying to get my homework done and I can't do it with you bothering me. Let me get it done and we'll play afterwards."

Some tips about I-Messages from *P.E.T.* by Thomas Gordon that can help a conductor with discussion after a roleplay:[7]

a. Watch for what seems to be an I-Message, but really is a You-Message. Example: "I get upset whenever *you* goof off."

b. Encourage players to accentuate the positive, not the negative in their I-Messages.

c. An I-Message will not work if the player understates how he feels. Encourage players to express emotion in the degree they are feeling it.

d. Watch for "I am angry" remarks. They are usually You-Messages for they are directed at someone else and are only a secondary feeling. A player's own embarrassment, hurt, disappointment, resentment, or needs may trigger an angry feeling, and he may direct it at an opponent in the roleplay. A blameless player may wonder what he has done to cause this.

15. Watch for the player who tries to take on the problems of the other players. He will tend to do this in real life. Like Atlas he is trying to carry the whole world on his shoulders. Both growth and dialogue are promoted in a mutual-rights environment. Every person has needs and rights, and when his needs are going unmet or his rights are abridged, he is said to have or to "own" the problem.[8] And it is up to *him* to find a solution. Sometimes one player will try to "own" another player's problem (this is scripted in RP 16, p. 114)—and this will prevent the real owner from coming to terms with it. With help, the roleplayers will learn to distinguish whose problem it is. When it is their problem, they will shoulder it. When it is not, they will recognize this and possibly learn better ways to help.

16. Watch for the player who does not finish a thought or a sentence before rushing on to his next idea. This quirk is confusing and a listener's reaction may be sharp or irritated.

17. Watch for the player (or member of the audience) with irritating habits that distract from the roleplaying. Some people have the habit of tapping a pencil or their feet, others of drumming their fingers. Still others keep watching the clock or glancing at their watch. Usually these actions indicate to the others that this person is bored. Such actions also indicate that the offending person is not bothering to listen very carefully. This is impolite if not rude. During the discussion find out if the offending person has been listening and ask the others how they feel about this inattention.

18. Watch for the player who has the bad habit of breaking in and finishing a sentence when he thinks he knows what the other person is going to say. He may be right, but right or wrong it is distracting to the speaker.

19. Watch for players who speak in a monotone, without expression or seemingly without energy. Are they finding it hard to gain their point? Modeling can be used here to advantage, to show how expression in a person's voice and some aliveness can get better results.

20. Words are only the stimulus or the symbol of the meaning underneath. Players should try to understand what another player is trying to say. Watch for the player who is taking the words literally, and makes no attempt to search for a meaning. He seems unable to "read between the lines." Sometimes a player will even say, "I don't care what you meant. What you *said* was . . . ."

21. Be aware of players who ask questions but will not accept the answers they are given. Some keep on asking the same question until they get the answer they want. This habit can be irritating and a new more acceptable way should be learned. (Young people acquire this habit from parents or teachers who use the device frequently.)

22. Look for manipulation. Not just the aggressive kind, but the soft-sell type: "You go ahead, Dear, and don't worry about poor little me." Watch for the player who plays the role like a wounded hero for all the mileage he can get. This is a form of manipulation; so is humility.

Watch for places where a player is being pressured or manipulated into another way of thinking. How does he react? Does he handle it quickly and easily? Does he handle it by using another type of manipulation? This should be brought up in the discussion session after the roleplay.

A book by Everett Shostrom, *Man, The Manipulator,* gives names to the types of manipulators. The entire book is worth reading for a roleplaying conductor. Shostrom's eight manipulative types are listed with the game "Manipulative Basketball" in chapter 4 (p. 63). After the manipulative game there is a list of traits which are typical of manipulation, along with their opposites—qualities characteristic of what we call "actualizing."

23. Watch for the conversational novice who does not know where and how to become a part of conversation. He breaks in at the wrong time and is hurt by the lack of response. You can help this reticent kind of person by putting him into a roleplay with more than two players.

24. Sometimes an aggressive player, in his desire to get his own point across, will completely ignore what the player before him said. If one player has ignored another several times, the conductor might stop the roleplaying and ask the ignored player how he is feeling.

25. There is a parent, adult, and child in every individual. At different times one or the other of these personal parts gets the upper hand and expresses itself in words and actions. In the teenager this is more noticeable than at any other time in life, for teenagers slip easily from the child to the adult and then back to the child—or perhaps to the parent. In roleplaying the conductor will become increasingly aware of when one of these states dominates his players. Berne, Harris, and James and Jongeward have made a study of these times (when one of the personality characteristics is predominant) and call them *Ego States*. PAC Pinball, a game in this book, (p. 98) is based on these Ego States and the reader may wish to refer to it for further knowledge on the subject when he begins to notice these states in his conducting.

26. Allow players the right to refuse a role, or to quit a role if it becomes too uncomfortable.

27. It will be obvious to the conductor that these roleplays can be used many times with the same players; they simply change the parts they play. It may *not* be as obvious that a player who was having trouble with a particular part could repeat it sometime later pitted against different players. In this way they learn new ways of reacting and gain proficiency in them.

These general instructions are important because with roleplays you are *not* dealing with just particular roles, but with *people* who are *roleplaying*. After each role suggestions of what to watch for are given. These are based on what will probably happen. But bear in mind that they are only suggestions. Some suggestions will apply for one playing of the role; other suggestions for another playing of the role with different players. It is possible to conceive of circumstances where none would apply. There would be nothing wrong with your conducting or with the role. It is just that in roleplaying you are dealing with unique and unpredictable people. Every one of these people has different experiences and feelings. The roleplay is just the setting, the situation, the start.

Keeping the above paragraph in mind, if the roleplay goes off on a wild tangent, allow it to continue as long as it remains vital. When it becomes bogged down and either the audience or the players lose interest, stop the playing and find out what has happened. It can then be gently brought back to problem solving, or ended because of the impossibility of a solution.

Suggested reading:

Muriel James and Dorothy Jongeward, *Born to Win* (Reading, Mass.: Addison-Wesley Publishing Co., 1971); and

Everett L. Shostrom, *Man, the Manipulator* (New York: Bantam Books, Inc., 1968).

3

listening

Dialogue is often impossible simply because we do not listen to what the other person is trying to say.

A friend of mine, a social worker and a very understanding person, finds it hard to forget a cry for help that she simply did not hear.

Just after getting home from a trip, my friend, Kitty, went over to get a parakeet she had left with a neighbor. After the usual small talk the woman asked her in an offhand manner, "Kitty, have you got a little time to talk? I've got . . . a . . . a problem I'd like to discuss with you."

Kitty was rushed (there were so many things she had to do because of being away) so she said, "Gosh Martha, I can't stop now, but I'll call you early tomorrow morning. Okay?"

That afternoon the woman went into a closet with a shotgun and blew her head off. Kitty said that Martha was a quiet person who talked very little, and she should have known that it was important. Very few of us would have heard that cry, but there are voices of people all around us that hide their desperate need.

The roles in this chapter deal with the different types of sensitive listening, from attention to "body language" to the type of listening that tries to hear the reason and the emotion behind the words.

23

FEAR OF CRITICISM, OR POOR LISTENING?

Roleplay 1

*Basil: Basil has been barking at everybody for days, mostly because he hasn't seen Mae since their quarrel of a couple of days ago. He misses her a lot but is almost too angry to talk to her. She rather bluntly suggested that he talk over their problems with *her* instead of running to his mother. He's no mama's boy and she knows it! His mother is a grand old gal and a guy needs a sympathetic listener. Would she rather he go to some girl? He knows plenty of takers in that category! If she would just keep her big mouth shut and listen once in a while instead of interrupting with stupid suggestions that would have no chance of working out. Like the stupid things she said when he had that run-in with his boss at his after-school job. What does she think he is—a nincompoop? Maybe he ought to date that quiet girl in his chemistry class!

Mae: Realizing she has spent very little time talking to her boyfriend in a personal way, Mae now is determined to find out why, even if it means another quarrel. And they've had plenty of those lately! Why does he seem to shy away from talks on their relationship? This time she's not going to be put off by his authoritarian tone or his big grandiose explanations. And she's not going to let his anger or sulking in silence bother her. She wishes she hadn't brought up the subject of his mother in their quarrel but she had resented his bringing in a third person. She wishes she didn't love the dope. No phone call in two days. Is he calling it off?

[As the scene opens, it is nine at night and the doorbell rings. Mae goes to the door and is surprised to find Basil. She invites him in.]

Mae: You've been avoiding me lately, Basil. Why?

Basil: I've been talking to my mother instead.

Mae: I'm sorry about that, Basil. No one likes to have their quarrels aired with other people.

Basil: Mother sensed we had a quarrel. I was just hoping she could help me understand something. Lately when we're together, I always end up feeling angry.

Mae: Always? Maybe you do it on purpose so you won't have to continue a conversation with me!

*Role-descriptions and dialogue are for the conductor only; they are given as guides.

Suggestions for the Roleplay "Fear of Criticism, or Poor Listening?"

Selecting Your Players. This roleplay pictures a girl who talks instead of listening and a boy who is a little too sensitive about criticism. However, you don't need players who show these characteristics obviously, since everyone has them to some degree. Players should be of equal fighting ability or as near to this as possible.

Instructions for Players. Remember, the descriptions and the role-dialogue are for the conductor. You should be trying to instill confidence in your players by sympathizing with each one in turn. To Basil you might say: "Who does Mae think she is, making cracks about your being a mama's boy! Is she just trying to get you sore?" Etc. To Mae you might say: "You wonder what's wrong with Basil lately. You're listening to some of his troubles and trying to help him and suddenly he's sore about something! If you didn't love him so much you'd tell him you never wanted to see him again!"

Remember to set the scene for your players so that they can more easily be a part of the role. The scene given here is only a suggestion. If another scene would have more meaning to the particular players you're working with, by all means use it. To bring Basil into the role you should add something like: "You know it's late but you've decided you *must* talk with Mae. You have gone over to her house and have rung the bell. Looking through the window, you see that she, and not her mother, is coming to answer the door." Then set the scene for Mae by something like: "The doorbell has just rung and you wonder who would be ringing it so late. You go to the door and there stands Basil."

What to Watch for. Sensitive listening and leveling are important here. The role-dialogue given shows how leveling moves the players closer to the problem if not always to the solution. It shows how the action moves forward when one player is able to swallow a nasty remark or a sarcastic one. The role-dialogue is also intended to show how careless words slow the action and how exaggeration tends to bring forth anger. These are some of the things you should be watching for so that you can bring them up in the discussion, or model a better way.

In modeling you might try Thomas Gordon's technique of "active listening," which he describes in his book *P.E.T.*[1] This is the kind of listening that gives a feedback on what the listener is hearing. In giving feedback, you should try to express what you feel is the emotional impact behind what the sender is saying. Suppose, for example, that Basil is telling how his employer yelled at him to pick up the bag of potatoes or growled at him when he entered a room. Active listening might be expressed by saying: "I gather what you're saying, Basil, is that you didn't mind his orders, but it's the way he gave them to you that you object to and that makes you angry." This is not offering advice, but just showing the other person that you are listening and understanding.

Discussion Following the Roleplay. The discussion is important especially to those playing the roles. If two casts are used, there should be a discussion after each roleplay. Each person in the cast should be allowed to give his feelings before the roleplay is opened up for general discussion. Ask each player in turn how he was feeling during the roleplay and at the end. Encourage everyone to discuss any problems they encountered. Sensitive and active listening is the keynote of this role. You should explain active listening, then give the members of the casts (and then the audience) a chance to state where they think this type of listening could have been used to advantage. Leveling is always important and, if possible, you, as conductor, should point out where active or sensitive listening helped free the other person so that he could level.

Games and discussion questions on listening are given at the end of this chapter. The game, "I-Thou Feedback" (p. 38), deals especially with active listening.

UNWARRANTED HELP

Roleplay 2

*Carol: Because she has never been able to make her mother understand her point of view, Carol realizes that more and more she has been going along with her mother's ideas. Today, she has brought home, on approval, a darling ankle-length skirt like the ones her friends are wearing. Her mother has expressed disapproval of the long-length style for afternoon wear. It is very important to Carol that she keep the skirt. More than the item of clothing is involved here!

Eve: The mother of Carol. Eve is a dominant woman who does not seem to understand her daughter. To her, Carol seems to have such a hard time making up her mind. Even when she does make it up, you can never be sure she won't change it a number of times. One should make a decision and go with it. But she's basically a sensible girl, not addicted to doing things like wearing ankle-length skirts to school.

[Scene opens when Carol comes into the living room carrying a box containing the skirt.]

Carol: Can we talk a little before dinner, Mother?

Mother: Of course, Dear. What's in the box?

Carol: I'll tell you about that later. First of all, I want to remind you that I'm almost as old as you were when you got married. It's about time I started making my own decisions, even if they're wrong!

Mother: I'm not trying to make your decisions for you, Carol.

Carol: Maybe not consciously. Remember the talk we had about the hours I was to be in on weekends?

Mother: Yes. You made a decision and then changed your mind.

Carol: No, Mother. *You* made the decision. I just got talked into it. I'll grant that it's your prerogative to set hours, but you're wrong about the time!

Mother: But you agreed!

Carol: No! I couldn't make you understand, so I gave in.

Mother: Eleven o'clock is late enough to be out. Twelve-thirty is ridiculous!

Carol: Ridiculous to you—not to me! I have my friends to deal with.

*Role-descriptions and dialogue are for the conductor's use only. They are given as guides.

Suggestions for the Roleplay "Unwarranted Help"

Selecting Your Players. This is a role for lightweight and heavyweight players. A dominant girl should play the role of the mother; a shy personality the daughter. If you are using two casts and you have players that are very obviously lightweight and heavyweight players, you may want to concentrate on the heavyweight in one cast and the lightweight in the other. In this case you would then have them opposed by players of normal "weight." Since the second cast will be out of the room when the first cast performs, it would be best to allow the lightweight to be in the first cast so she can learn by watching how someone else plays her role.

Instructing Your Players. Remember you are *not* instructing your players in what they are to say or how they should feel, but in what they should know. In this case, they should *not* know they are playing the role of a lightweight or a heavyweight. If one asks, "How do I start?", you can counter by telling her to do what she normally would do. If that is by saying nothing, and just sitting there, allow her to do it, for that is probably what a shy person would do. It will be up to the other person to break the ice. If they both sit there and say nothing, allow it to remain that way for a time. Plays sometimes start in this way. Do not allow your audience to make fun of the players! This is important for teenagers. It is one of the main reasons why someone with authority should be conducting the roleplaying. Equally important is that your audience be composed *only* of those who will be roleplaying. To Carol, the daughter, after giving her some of the facts, you could say: "No matter what happens, you are going to keep that skirt. You have promised yourself this." To Eve, the mother, you can say: "Your daughter has such a hard time making a decision. And even then she doesn't stick with it! Why is it so hard for you to understand your daughter? You don't have this trouble with your son." Encourage your players to use other things besides the skirt that have personal meaning for them.

Remember, after giving your instructions you must set the scene for each of your players. It does not have to be complicated or long; just be sure to give them enough background to plunge them into the situation—so they feel a part of it. To Carol, the daughter, you could say something like: "You pick up the box with the skirt and go into the living room where your mother is sitting reading the paper." To Eve, the mother, it might be: "Your daughter has just entered the room with an odd expression on her face. She is carrying a box that looks as if it might contain clothes of some kind. You put down your paper wondering what the box contains."

What to Watch for. The dialogue given here (besides expanding the plot) shows the aim and direction of the roleplay. Both players should be using sensitive listening so that each can understand the other's point of view. Active listening—which goes beyond the words to the meaning and emotions behind them—can be used to advantage here. Are your players using any form of it? Do your players seem to be sensitive to each other's facial expressions and tone of voice?

Watch for defensive actions on the part of the lightweight player. How does she handle aggression? When backed against a wall, how does she react? The dialogue given here shows how the daughter can handle the situation firmly without resorting to any defensive actions such as put-downs or biting remarks. Does the lightweight player sound as if she believed in the facts? Does she present her facts in a low-key manner seemingly without energy? Watch for the heavyweight who comes on so strong that the lightweight is not allowed even breathing room.

Leveling is important here, for unless the lightweight tells how she feels and the heavyweight gives her reaction, arriving at a solution is difficult.

Discussion Following the Roleplay. The discussion will depend a great deal on how the role was played. Your dominant character may not have been as aggressive as you expected. She should then be told that she played the role with sensitiveness to the needs of the other person. If aggressive, she should be told (as was mentioned above in the general suggestions) that winning is not the most important item in interpersonal relations, and that she might try tying her hand behind her back, figuratively speaking. (This should be done tactfully, perhaps even speaking to the heavyweight privately, so as not to make the shy person uncomfortable.) If the lightweight player was unable to keep her vow of not giving up the skirt, the conductor might try helping her by modeling the role with her opponent.

DRUGS AND LISTENING

Roleplay 3

*Mike: A thirteen-year-old boy who has just been dismissed from school for smoking marihuana. He has been walking around trying to figure out a way to explain to his parents what happened. Will they understand that he needed to be a part of the gang? Could he get by with telling them it was just the first time? What if they found out about the pills?

Beth: A woman about thirty-five. She is horrified when the school phones and tells her that her son has been caught smoking marihuana. He was dismissed from school early but has not come home. She blames her husband for always being too busy to take an interest in the boy. Was smoking pot all that was involved?

Bart: Alarmed when his wife calls and tells him their son has been dismissed from school for smoking marihuana. On the way home he remembers when he sneaked a smoke behind the garage. But not marihuana! He is surprised that his son is old enough to smoke—or want to! He had been thinking of him as a baby. He realizes that he does not know his son.

[Mike walks into the living room to find both of his parents waiting for him. He can tell by their expressions that the school has called.]

Mike: I suppose the school has called?

Father: Yes, Son. Can you tell us about it?

Mike: Look, it's no big deal, Dad. I just had to show the guys I wasn't afraid. Wouldn't you know I'd get caught on my first attempt?

Father: I can see that it's important for you to be a part of the gang and be accepted by your peers, Mike.

Mike: Yeah, Dad. I felt kinda left out. Then, I . . . .

Mother: It would have been better for you to have been left out of *that* gang, entirely! I don't approve of some of the boys Mike calls his friends, Bart.

Mike: Who do you mean?

Mother: Guy and Bob. I understand from some of the P.T.A. mothers that they're using harder drugs. What have you got to say about that, young man?

*Role-descriptions and dialogue are for the conductor only; they are given as guides.

Suggestions for the Roleplay "Drugs and Listening"

Selecting Your Players. Your players' fighting abilities should be about equal, but the role can be played with any "weights." Try to compensate for a lightweight with more instructions. Any sex can play the boy part. The parent roles are not prop roles (i.e., simply used as foils) but are dealing with the Parent Ego State of the players (parent within the players).

Instructing Your Players. Remember, the descriptions and role-dialogue are only for the conductor. You will be addressing your players in the second person in your own words, and trying to give them confidence in the role they are to play. To the boy, Mike, you can say: "What are you worried about? This should be no big deal. Marihuana is certainly no worse than whiskey and both your parents drink. They couldn't have found the 'uppers' or that joint you sewed in your coat or they'd have said something about it, wouldn't they?" Remember to bring the boy-player into the role as you finish: "You see your Dad's car is home so they are probably waiting. Might as well get it over with! You walk in and can tell by their expressions that they know." To the mother, Beth, you could say something like: "It's Bart's fault! If he had taken more interest in the boy this wouldn't have happened. You've had a funny feeling for some time that something was wrong." Etc. To plunge her into the scene you can say: "Well, here's Mike and he does look worried. Is it more than marihuana?"

Remember, you must give certain facts, such as the boy's being dismissed from school for smoking marihuana, but each player should be given a little different slant with some other facts. To the father, Bart, you might say: "Your business has put such demands on your time that you haven't had a chance to know the boy. But boys will be boys. Isn't Beth making too much of the whole deal?" And to get him into the scene: "Here is Mike now and he does look worried. But who wouldn't be?—sent home in disgrace, getting bawled out by the principal and now about to get bawled out again."

What to Watch for. The start of the role-dialogue given here shows that no matter how gently the parents begin, the boy will be put on the defensive. Sensitive listening and gentle questioning are necessary here to allow the boy-player to be free to level. (Not only about the other drugs he is taking but about some of the deeper feelings the player might think caused it.) If the boy-player can be made to feel he is getting both understanding and love, he is more likely to want to level.

Gordon's "active listening" mentioned above (where the listener gives feedback on what he thinks the feeling is behind the sender's words) could be used to advantage here. The father in the role-dialogue here is showing this. Watch for the players who use some version of it, and others who talk instead of listening. Look for the players who sit and listen without giving any feedback on what they are hearing—not even a reaction. The player of the boy-part may interpret

31

this as anger or condemnation on the part of the parent-players. This will make him feel even more uneasy. Watch out also for the boy-player who feels that the sensitive listening should all be on the side of the parents and does not listen to what they are trying to say. Active listening should always be given a chance to go both ways. With a feeling of rebellion a player can be closing off the love and understanding he is getting from the other players.

Although the role-dialogue given here shows the father exercising caution and the mother coming on strong, watch for authoritarianism in either of the parent-players. Young people tend to parrot their parents in playing a parent role. This will take place not only in the roleplay but also in real life when the youth-player has children of his own. This is the parent input of the PAC (parent, adult, child) concept of Berne and Harris, mentioned above (see p. 20). Watch to see if both of the parent-players are going deep enough to discover all the facts.

Before the role is considered complete, some knowledge of the extra drugs should be brought out and the boy's reason for using them. If the boy refuses to tell about the capsule drugs, the conductor can fake a phone call from the principal of the school who says he has just heard it rumored that the boy has hard drugs sewed into the lining of his coat and the parents should check it out. The conductor could also send in another player (a prop player) who would volunteer the information.

Discussion Following the Roleplay. Sensitive listening and leveling are again the keynotes. The players should be asked how they were feeling and what caused them to respond the way they did. Bring up what you have observed of the parent input or the Parent Ego State of the parent-players. There can be some discussion on this, since the parent-players may not realize why they played the roles as they did.

Active listening should be explained. If any of the players has used a version of it, this should be brought out. Explain that this type of listening can show the other person you are trying hard to understand what he is telling you. If leveling has been a factor in the roleplay, bring out where it helped and where the lack of it slowed down the action. If an aggressive manipulation was used bring this out in the discussion.

The players and the audience may like to practice some of the listening games explained at the end of this chapter. After the games the young people may like to try another role that requires sensitive or active listening.

(Although the role is written primarily for teenagers, a conductor might also like to use it with *parents* who are having trouble with their teenagers. Have someone else besides their own child play the boy-role. It can be played by anyone of any age or sex. Watch for authoritarianism then, and for conflict between the parents that slows the action.)

32

THIS CRAZY WORLD

Roleplay 4

*Pricilla: A conservative girl of sixteen raised in a strict religious family, Pricilla felt out of place with her childhood girl friends because they were always talking about the pill and experiments with sex. She found the talk distasteful and said so. Because they seemed sex-mad to her, she had been spending a lot of time with a mannish girl who didn't date but was interesting to talk to and excellent at all sports. Her former friends started teasing her about having "gay" tendencies. Ignoring it at first, she began to wonder if they could be right, for she *was* repelled when a date made an awkward pass. Of the boys she dated she liked her chemistry partner the best; he was fun to be with and talked about other things besides sex. As her worry about being gay increased, she encouraged him and began to date him steadily. Her girl friends were delighted and she found she had missed being a part of their group. But she felt uncomfortable and false, so she deliberately tried sex, only to find that she didn't like it. Her fear of having gay tendencies is becoming an obsession, and, added to that, she realizes she's pregnant. She doesn't want to get married and abortion would be no simple matter in her family. Her life is a mess and there is no one she can talk to. Is suicide the only answer?

Grandmother: Sixty-five-year-old woman who lives near her children and grandchildren and loves them deeply. But they are busy living active lives and she has been lonely. Now she is thinking of doing something that's guaranteed to alienate them. She has formed a warm friendship with a gentleman friend and they are thinking of living together without benefit of marriage. If she got married she would lose her first husband's Social Security check, and she and her friend would not have enough to live on without it. Would she miss her relationship with her family and be lonelier without them than she is now? Pricilla is her favorite and not as conservative as the rest. But will her tolerance of the new ways extend to her grandmother?

[As the scene opens, Pricilla has just come home from school to find her grandmother wandering around the house wondering where everybody is.]

Pricilla: Oh Gran, I'm so glad you're here! [hugs her with great enthusiasm] The family has gone to a potluck supper at the church. We'll fix something for ourselves and have a ball!

*Role-descriptions and dialogue are for the conductor only; they are given as guides.

Grandmother: Bless your heart, my Dear. [hugs her in return] It's so good to be here with you!

Pricilla: C'mon into the kitchen. We'll start things rolling. [leads the way to the kitchen]

Grandmother: [following her into the kitchen] How come you aren't with the family tonight?

Pricilla: I knew I'd be late getting home. [pause, low tone] That was just an excuse. I didn't want to go.

Grandmother: There must be a good reason why you didn't want to go. Do you think you could tell me?

Pricilla: [getting out some pans] I've got some problems that don't seem to have a solution.

Grandmother: In the past we've sometimes been able to figure out a way together. Remember that Girl Scout camp you wanted to go to? [pause, gentle tone] Do you think you might try telling me?

Pricilla: [moving pan to stove and emptying the contents of a plastic dish into pan] I don't know, Gran. I think this is somehow out of your league.

Grandmother: It could be a problem I haven't experienced. [pause] Even when I haven't known the answer, I've known where to find it. Haven't I?

Pricilla: Yes you have. [long pause]

Grandmother: Once when I was a girl and out with a new boy, I was with a group I didn't know and frankly didn't like. The petting went on quite far before I could stop it. A couple of weeks later my period didn't come. I was frantic. I wasn't sure anything had happened, but then I wasn't sure it hadn't!

Pricilla: [with obvious interest] What did you do, Gran?

Grandmother: I went to the library. I wasn't sure the librarian believed my story about a term paper but I didn't care. After a long search I found my answer. It was probably anxiety that caused the period to be late.

Pricilla: Gosh, Gran, do you think the library would have anything about homosexuals?

Suggestions for the Roleplay "This Crazy World"

Selecting Your Players. Youths of any fighting ability can play the roles. The part of the grandmother is not a prop role and will bring out the Parent Ego State of the player. This is a role without conflict and the emphasis is on sympathetic listening and understanding.

Instructions for Players. Personalize your remarks to your players and let them feel your sympathy. To the grandmother you could say: "This younger generation is supposed to be open-minded about sex life, but does that extend to having a grandmother living with a man without sanction of marriage?" Etc. Inform the grandmother-player that she has a good relationship with Pricilla because she has used her own experiences from her early life to help the girl. But caution your player against giving judgmental examples. Finish your instructions with a remark that brings your player right into the act like: "You have gone over to your daughter's house to tell the family of your circumstances, only to find no one home. You are about to leave when Pricilla walks in."

To help Pricilla you could say: "You've tried but found you couldn't talk to your father or mother. And your minister? He's living in the dark ages and probably doesn't know what the word *gay* means." Etc. Then set the scene: "You have come home from school to find your grandmother wondering where everybody is. The family won't be home for some time—they are at a potluck supper at church—and you are glad. Your grandmother is a great gal and you have a good relationship with her."

What to Watch for. Leveling is important here and it may be difficult for the Pricilla-player to bring out all the facts. Watch for facts that are ignored or brought out reluctantly. The emphasis in this role is on sensitive listening and gut-level sympathy. Is the grandmother-player helping the girl-player to feel enough at ease so that she can level? Is she giving some experiences from her own life or that of her friends? Do they apply to the age of the granddaughter?

The start of the role-conversation here shows Pricilla's love for her grandmother, and it sets the tone for a good confidential talk. This is one way an outgoing personality can help a type who finds it hard to show feelings. The leveling in the role-dialogue given shows how the problem can be brought into the open quickly. Sensitive listening, gentle persuasion, and physical contact are also shown in the role-dialogue here.

Discussion Following the Roleplay. Find out from the girl-player whether or not she was feeling the sympathetic listening of the grandmother-player. Did the grandmother-player use any physical contact? If not, why not? Did the grandmother-player's examples of experiences from her early life (or experiences made up from a friend's experiences or knowledge gained in reading) help the girl-player? Were all the facts brought out? If some facts have been forgotten, is there a reason? If it can be done in a helpful way discuss abortion and suicide. Discuss homosexuality. The role tries to show that a lack of knowledge about what is "gay" is one reason for the problem. Games at the end of this chapter and chapter 6 on love can be used to advantage here.

Games That Can Be Played with Chapter 3

MIMIC CHARADES

Game 1

"Body language," that is, a player's expression and his body movements, can tell a great deal more than people realize. Your eyes may be getting a more accurate message than your ears. Sensitive listening includes receiving this non-verbal communication. Here is a game to help players become sensitized to this form of listening and to be aware of all the ways in which we express ourselves. It is a variation of charades.

The game is played by choosing up teams of from five to ten players. (If the group is very large the teams may be larger.) The teams should have a name and a motto to intensify the competition.

When teams are ready each team sends a representative to the conductor. He then gives each representative a word which they take back to their teams and act out in pantomime. Unlike regular charades, the players will be unable to use the sign language for syllables (long and short, cut-off, and so on). The word must be shown entirely by actions or facial expressions. When a team has guessed the word, the representative quickly raises her hand. The first team to guess gets three points, the second team two, and the third team one.

Then another representative from each team goes up to receive a word, and so on. When one team completes a set of words or reaches twenty points (or any other amount the conductor chooses), the game will be declared at an end and the winning team given proper commendation.

Example: After receiving the word, the representative will go back to his or her team and demonstrate picking up a jar and screwing off the cover. The player sets the cover down and reaches into the jar, bringing out something she puts in her mouth. Her face will register a sour taste—but one she likes! The word she had been given is, of course, *pickle*. (This is only one of many ways the word can be acted out.)

The conductor can select any words and any number of words for the game. They can relate to each other or (for more difficulty) be unrelated. The conductor should start with words easy to mimic and then increase their difficulty.

Some sets of words are (pick some from each list for an unrelated set):

violin	basketball	pickle
accordion	tennis racket	lemon
piano	skates	bitter pill
drums	baseball bat	spoon of castor oil
tambourine	golf club	onion
bass fiddle	sled	corn
xylophone	baseball	apple
organ	hockey stick	peach
saxophone	golf ball	walnut
banjo	skis	a grape
zither	ski pole	mango
boots	rocker	clown
pantyhose	typewriter	acrobat
girdle	car	lion tamer
belt	chair	ringmaster
coat	door	circus horseback rider
overshoes	book	circus barker
bathrobe	bed	horse rider on merry-go-round
parka	lamp	tightrope walker
wet socks	clock	Ferris wheel rider
purse	dictionary	trapeze artist
dress	table	circus

I-THOU FEEDBACK
(An Active Listening Game)

Game 2

AIM: To promote better listening.

PLAYERS: Pair players off, preferably with a boy and girl in each pair. Place your players in chairs facing each other.

SETTING: Pleasant room devoid of distractions such as disturbing noises, drafts, room too hot or too cold, etc. (Or as close to this as possible.)

Instructions for Speaker:

Have the speaker choose a subject or topic that he feels deeply about, and which has some emotional overtones for him (if possible). Or have the speaker choose a controversial subject on which he has a strong viewpoint.

Examples: Living together without marriage
Cheating on tests
Abortion for teenage girls
Use of the pill for teenagers
Dirty politics
Double standard for premarital sex
Legalization of marihuana
Older brothers and sisters

Instructions for Listener:

This is a game on listening so impress upon your audience the need for listening carefully to all your instructions. These are important because they are blocks to listening.

1. Explain that most physical distractions have been eliminated, but that players will have to use rigid discipline for a short time to rid themselves of other distractions, such as:

    a. Watching clock, fiddling with keys or other objects, pencil tapping, etc.

    b. Desire to daydream

    c. Desire or compulsion to think of problems of the day or worries, etc.

The listener should:

2. Give full physical attention. He should sit up straight and look directly at partner. This is supposed to keep a listener alert and free from distractions.

3. Watch for the "body language" of the speaker, his gestures, grimaces, and the pitch, tone and volume of his voice. Words alone do not tell the whole tale.

4. Note any omissions the speaker makes since understanding often comes from these omissions.

5. Be as open-eared and as open-minded as possible. The listener must rid himself of any negative feelings he might have for the speaker.

6. Gain as close a rapport with his partner as he can. He must try to achieve empathy! Have him make a heroic effort to understand what the speaker is saying (or trying to say!), and why he feels the way he does.

7. Be careful to avoid being so overstimulated by a word or so repelled by a point of view that he forgets to listen.

8. Be sensing and interpreting as the speaker-partner is talking, so that he can demonstrate acceptance in the form of feedback. This does not mean he has to agree with him, only that he show his partner he is listening and is "with him" and "on target."

9. Keep in mind the purpose for listening. In this case it is the gist of what the partner is saying (or trying to say), and the reason for the emotion behind it (if there is any and if it can be figured out).

First step is the SPEAKER'S DISCOURSE:

The conductor will explain that the speaker will have about a minute to talk on his favorite subject, during which the listener will give his full attention. After the minute is up the conductor will call, "time's up!"

Second step is the FEEDBACK that the LISTENER will give:

The listener will give the speaker feedback on what he thought the speaker was saying and meaning. If emotion is observed, and the listener has some understanding of what caused it, he should try to indicate that he understands the reason for it. Encourage the listener to achieve empathy if possible.

Thomas Gordon, who developed "active listening," advises his participants to avoid these typical twelve points in using feedback technique:[2]

    1. Ordering, directing, commanding.
    2. Warning, admonishing, threatening.
    3. Exhorting, moralizing, preaching.
    4. Advising, giving solutions or suggestions.
    5. Lecturing, teaching, giving logical arguments.
    6. Judging, criticizing, disagreeing, blaming.
    7. Praising, agreeing.
    8. Name calling, ridiculing, shaming.
    9. Interpreting, analyzing, diagnosing.
   10. Reassuring, sympathizing, consoling.
       ("Things will be better" or "I used to go through that too.")
   11. Probing, questioning, interrogating.

12. Withdrawing, distracting, humoring, diverting.
    ("Just forget about it" or "Let's talk about something else.")

Third step is the SPEAKER'S REACTION:

When the listener has given his feedback, the speaker will correct it or indicate it is all right. He will then rate the listener with one or two points for good and very good feedback, or four points for excellence.

Then the players will reverse roles and repeat. After each player has had a chance to be both speaker and listener, the players will shift chairs to get new partners, and then repeat the game. This can be repeated as long as the game holds interest and time permits. If a player complains that a partner is not being fair with his points, a game can be played with a third person as an observer.

The player with the most points wins.

Listing as a Discussion Technique:

LISTENING
(to be used for the roleplaying discussions)

A. When does a person listen best?
   *1. When he is interested in the subject or has a compelling reason to know information.
   2. When distractions are minimized or when he has trained himself to eliminate distractions.
   3. When taking notes. Why?
      a. Because the act improves attentiveness.
      b. Listener is able to review what he has heard.
      c. Notes remedy weaknesses in listener's ability to learn from spoken word.

B. List bad habits that discourage listening.[3]
   1. Faking attention and not trying to understand.
   2. Being so concerned with facts that you miss what they're leading to.
   3. Trying so hard to memorize some facts that you miss others.
   4. Avoiding difficult listening. (TV-type of listening is so habitual that you're unwilling to make extra effort when more is required.)
   5. Dismissing the subject as uninteresting.
   6. Using speaker's appearance or poor delivery as an excuse for not listening.
   7. Yielding to distractions. (Draft, noise, etc.)

C. Why is *critical* listening difficult? (Why is it hard to combat salesmen, rumors, politicians?)[4]
   1. Time element. No time to analyze.
   2. Oral persuasion more effective.
   3. Spoken word not as accurate. It can be colored with humor or pathos.
   4. Drop defenses in a chance encounter; there is no motive to be critical.
   5. Person-to-person relationships promote trust.
   6. Blinded by labels that produce emotion.
   7. Intrigued by idea of exclusive information or "inside dope."
   8. When hearing many good points, you forget to be critical or look for bad points.

*The answers given are only suggestions. Have your players give their own answers, and do not give suggestions unless it is absolutely necessary.

41

9. Tendency to follow the crowd.
10. Sympathetic to someone like us. A "good Joe."
11. Attracted by the glamor of someone well known in a field or an authority on a subject.

D. List barriers to listening.
1. Words have different meanings to different people.
2. Language and other differences in social or cultural backgrounds.
3. Not trying to understand. Tuned out.
4. Have values different from speaker's. (Object to the views expressed.)
5. Dislike speaker or feel resentment toward him.
6. Words loaded with emotion tend to tune you out from rest of speech.
7. Speaker has nervous mannerisms. (Jingles money, glances away from audience, etc.)
8. Speaker doesn't speak clearly. (Poor enunciation, mumbling, slurring, etc.)
9. Speaker talks too softly or too loudly, or in an annoying tone.
10. Listener has preconceptions, lacks attention, notices interruptions.
11. Objects in speaker's mouth make it hard to understand. (Pipe, cigarette, gum, etc.)
12. Speaker doesn't look directly at listener or audience.
13. Speaker's words are not meaningful to listener.
14. Speaker sends indirect messages that repel.
15. Speaker uses put-downs, judgmental statements, sarcasm, name calling, prejudices that produce anger.
16. Speaker shows dogmatism or argumentativeness.
17. Speaker talks too much and too fast.

E. What are the three most important things for listening?
1. *Discipline.* Listening is an art like music or painting and the discipline must come from within. It is necessary to listening.
2. *Concentration.* Listening is hard and demands an active participation and a relaxed alertness.
3. *Comprehension.* Necessary to understand and grasp the idea or meaning of what is heard. This should be the intent of both the sender and receiver, for a good listener joins the speaker in the excursion of understanding.

Take Note:

These listings are to help the teenagers form an idea and express it as concisely as possible. Too often teenagers' stumbling attempts and vague ideas are met with put-downs or ignored. The conductor can pick up these vague ideas, and (with or without the help of the suggestions) bring the ideas into focus with the question. He can then write them briefly on the blackboard.

Haim Ginott, in his book *Between Parent and Teenager*, says we: *win a teen-ager's attention* when we listen and respond sympathetically, *win his heart* when we express for him clearly what he said vaguely, *win his respect* when we are authentic and our words fit our feeling.[5]

Suggested reading:

Thomas Gordon, *P. E. T., Parent Effectiveness Training* (New York: Peter H. Wyden, Inc., 1970);
Ralph G. Nichols and Leonard A. Stevens, *Are You Listening?* (New York: McGraw-Hill Book Co., 1957).

4

understanding

Failure to communicate is often—too often—caused by a lack of understanding. Paul Tournier, in his book *To Understand Each Other*, tells us that to understand is to love and that a person who feels understood feels loved.[1]

The roleplays in this chapter attempt to get at some basics of understanding by showing how everyone approaches problems from a different angle. Remember the story of the four blind men approaching an elephant from different angles. Using their hands to see instead of their eyes, one described his trunk, another his ears, and the other two his body and a leg. Although their descriptions varied a great deal, together they gave a fairly accurate picture of an elephant.

The roles in this chapter aim at getting the players to look at problems from perspectives other than their own. To do this the player is put in a situation where the conflict is best resolved by understanding something of his opponent's way of looking at an issue.

EXTROVERT *vs* INTROVERT

Explanation of Types:

EXTROVERT:[2] Extroverts like people and like to be out in the bright lights with crowds, gaiety, and movement. They always have something to say and love to retell a story. Absorbed in events and in getting things done, they sometimes overdo almost to the point of exhaustion. Extroverted types work out their frustrations by action. They are sociable, cheerful, friendly, and tend to take a positive attitude. An extreme extrovert tends to avoid introspection and may even think it unhealthy.

INTROVERT: Introverts keep their best qualities to themselves and only show their gifts in sympathetic surroundings. They are over-conscientious and tend to be pessimistic, reacting to a new idea with a definite "no."[3] Introverted types are happy sitting alone in the dim light of an open fire or curled up with a good book. They look inward at their own ideals and goals. Interested in what an event really means, they love to evaluate it. They are the inventors, planners, and theorists. An extreme introvert is a passive person and tends to put off or avoid action.[4]

Roleplay 5 (the above Types personified in a situation):

*Elmo: A high school senior running for president of his class. He has enjoyed the campaigning, going around greeting old friends and making new ones. His girl, Lee, whom he had taken with him wherever he could, has been acting strange. He missed her the other night and found her out in the garden—alone! And the weather was cold! She sure was a strange girl, but she fascinated him.

Lee: A sophomore who has been very proud to be known as Elmo's girl. But she can't stand any more parties! She has a desperate need to relax and collect her thoughts. She enjoys being with Elmo, but whether he joins her or not, tonight she is determined to stay home.

[Elmo walks into Lee's house without knocking (as he always does) and late (as he usually is). He is horrified to find Lee in a housecoat.]

---

*Role-descriptions and dialogue are for the conductor only; they are given as guides.

Elmo: Gosh, Lee, don't you know we haven't got a second to spare? You're not dressed!

Lee: I'm not going, Elmo. With school every day and a party every night, I haven't had a chance to catch my breath, much less think. Oh Elmo, it'll be fun to stay home tonight. We haven't had a chance to talk together, alone, for a long time. We could have a fire.

Elmo: (starts to move around and talk rapidly) So we've been out a lot lately. You sound as if parties were hard work!

Suggestions for Roleplay "Extrovert *vs* Introvert"

Selecting Your Players. Selection is important in this role, because one who understands how an extrovert or introvert feels will more readily fight for that viewpoint. The selecting can be done in different ways. The simplest way would be to read the explanation given for the extrovert and introvert (but not the role-description or role-dialogue!) and have members of the audience volunteer for the part that seems closest to them. (You should explain that most people have some characteristics of both the extrovert and the introvert but more of a tendency towards one or the other.) For this role the players should be of equal fighting ability if possible, but identification with the role is more important.

Instructions for Players. You will be addressing each player in your own words and in the second person, so with "body language" and tone of voice you should instill some sympathy for the individual role he or she is to play. Part of what you could say to Lee, the girl part, might be: "Does he really love you if he would rather spend his time at parties talking to other people?" And to bring her into the role say something like: "You hear the car, the door slam, and here he is in a hurry as usual." To Elmo, the boy part, you could say: "From something Lee said, you gather she isn't too crazy about going to the party tonight. What cooks with this woman? She objects to parties and having fun?" To bring him into the role you could say: "You walk into her house and there she stands obviously not ready for the party."

You are trying to heighten the conflict between the players. Think of the program on television some time ago where the moderator would give his contestants conflicting stories. Before he threw them into the situation, he would turn to the audience and say, "Aren't we devils?" He knew what would bring controversy. If you know your players, there is a great deal you can add to increase the conflict.

What to Watch for. In this role each player should be working toward understanding the other person. Each should be trying to see how the situation looks from his opponent's point of view. They should work toward some kind of compromise where both can be happy. Take note of manipulating tactics. Look

47

for both the hard and soft sell. Watch for leveling. When both can state how they feel, the role will move faster. Your players may not understand each other and may not want to compromise. This need not continue too long, for you can stop the roleplaying and ask the players how they are feeling. If their trouble lies in not seeing each other's viewpoint, you might model for the player needing help. You could show how a great deal more can be accomplished by using understanding and some willingness to compromise. Nevertheless, the person may still not want to compromise. Don't push it too hard; nothing should be forced in roleplaying.

Discussion Following the Roleplay. After the roleplay, you should ask each player in turn how he or she was feeling during the playing and at the end. Encourage your players to bring up any problems they have encountered. Occasionally a player suffers a crushing defeat through no fault of his own but simply because the other player is rigid and will not budge. If he feels sensitive about it, he should be reassured, for he has been under a handicap. Remember that in each playing of these roles you are encountering something different. This is because the players are different. Their reactions to what is said (triggered by their past experience) will be unpredictable.

If you have two casts playing the role, you can ask the audience, after the second playing, to compare how the different players handled the situation. Did the players level about how they really felt? Did each one try to understand his opponent's view or did they all only cherish their own? Did any of them impose his views on the other player?

Tournier, in his book *To Understand Each Other,* says that men are attracted to their opposite in a woman (and *vice versa*), and that one of the purposes of marriage is to allow the two, through their close relationship, to discover and understand what they have not known before.[5] The audience may wish to test this with their own experiences of what attracts them to the opposite sex.

INTUITION *vs* SENSATION[6]

Explanation of the Functions:

INTUITION: Intuition tells you "what may be" and Uncle Hunch will play this part. He is an adventurous fellow alive with new ideas that have unlimited possibilities in the near future. At home with the invisible perception of ideas, he just seems to know something is right and reasons from there. Security (in the sense of certainty of outcome and realized potentials) stifles him. He has instinctive or psychic insight which he uses for his inventions.

SENSATION: Sensation tells you something "exists." Aunt Fact will take that role. She is an accurate observer who is convinced of the reality of the five senses. Being a worrier, she must be absolutely sure of any new undertaking or she is frantic with anxiety. She will scientifically bring in all the facts before any decision is made. She is a practical person.

Roleplay 6 (the above functions personified in a situation):

*Uncle Hunch: He has decided to sell some income property because he is off to new horizons and property is just a drag to take care of. It interferes with his work on his inventions.

Aunt Fact: Wife of Uncle Hunch whose name is Constance. She knows that this income property takes very little time to take care of and furnishes security for the present and future. She is in a very real panic at the thought of its being sold. He needs her signature on the deed to the property.

[Hunch has just come in the kitchen door all excited because he has a buyer for his income property. Aunt Fact continues with the dishes.]

Uncle Hunch: Constance Honey, I've got a buyer for the apartments!

Aunt Fact: Oh Hunch, don't you think we ought to talk this over a little more? I've been reading some statistics in the paper . . . .

Uncle Hunch: I don't care about any old statistics. I have a whole new project coming up and I can't be bothered playing nursemaid to apartments.

Aunt Fact: You seem to feel very strongly about this.

Uncle Hunch: I do, Constance. Those apartments stifle me. I need to be free.

---

*Role-descriptions and dialogue are for conductor only; they serve as a guide.

Aunt Fact: I can see that. What if I were to help with them? Doing the cleaning and renting?

Uncle Hunch: Well . . . . Why should you want to?

Aunt Fact: I have a desperate need for security, Hunch, and those apartments furnish it.

Uncle Hunch: That's foolish, Constance. You know that!

Aunt Fact: Maybe. But that's the way I feel. I can do the painting, Hunch. We could hire someone to do the things I couldn't.

Uncle Hunch: There's no need for you to work. I'll see that we have enough money! This new invention—

Aunt Fact: Where have I heard that before!

Uncle Hunch: So you've heard it before. My mind's made up. I'm going to sell whether you like it or not.

Aunt Fact: Have you forgotten that you need my signature on the deed?

Suggestions for Personification Roleplay "Intuition *vs* Sensation"

Selecting Your Players. The selection of players is also very important here because the player who has a natural feeling for his role can more easily fight for this view in a conflict. If your players are having trouble understanding what the Intuitive Function is, even after you've read the explanation of the Function, you might suggest some TV detective heroes who go about solving mysteries by playing a hunch. Dr. Gannon on *Medical Center* often uses educated intuitiveness in diagnosing his patients. And, just as often, he is in conflict with a doctor who is more concerned with just the facts before him. This latter doctor, who feels that Gannon's diagnosis is not warranted by the facts, is using the Sensation Function. The player's identification with the role is more important than his fighting ability.

Instructions for Players. In these personifying roles, you should try to make sure the player feels that the Type or Function he is playing is worthwhile and something he is proud of. In this particular role the Intuitive Function is being shown in the person of an inventor; he is unconcerned with security and hardly knows the meaning of the word. He represents the extreme. Our society has a strong tendency to belittle or dismiss impractical inventors, so your player may feel uncomfortable taking this part. (On the other hand, it has become fashionable to scorn middle-class securities, and adolescence is naturally a rebellious age, so your player may feel comfortable in the role.) If you sense (here, or with any of the personifications) that your player is feeling anxious or insecure because of the role, take time to dispel such a feeling. Explain that the capacity to go out to

50

a problem in an intuitive way is useful in all creative work, especially quantum physics. All innovators and inventors should be considered in the same light. You could also bring up the detective heroes, Dr. Gannon, etc.

To help Hunch, you could say: "What's with this woman? Does she want to tie you down to some stupid apartments when you have this important invention that needs your whole effort? Doesn't she understand your need to be free?" Remember to bring him into the roleplay with something like: "You have just come from the realtor's and you've found out they may have a buyer for the apartments. You open the door and hurry into the kitchen where you know you'll find Constance. There she is and you can't wait to tell her the good news."

To Aunt Fact, who is a practical person, you could say: "Doesn't Hunch understand your need for security? He's always off with something new like a little boy with a new toy." To bring Aunt Fact into the role: "You are doing dishes in the kitchen worrying about the apartment building's being up for sale. You hear Hunch's car and you can tell by his step he's happy about something. He bursts into the room, all smiles."

Bear in mind you are only trying to provide as much conflict as you can. It is up to the players to deal with the conflict and come up with ideas for compromise.

What to Watch for. In this role each player should be working toward understanding the point of view of the other person. This does not mean giving in to the other player's demands without fighting for some rights of your own. Hunch should understand his wife's need for security and try out some things in the way of compromise. Aunt Fact should realize Hunch's need to be free to go on to more creative ideas, and she should offer to compromise if he will forgo selling. Each should take a try at understanding and be able to give a little. Is either player taking an uncompromising attitude that cuts off dialogue? In the role-dialogue given here Hunch takes a hard line—almost with the first statement. Aunt Fact counters this beginning with calm, and with active listening, giving Hunch the freedom to level about how he feels. Watch to see if each of your players levels about how he or she feels so that the other player can begin to understand.

Is either of the players so interested in his own view that he doesn't listen to his opponent and sense his opponent's needs? When Hunch, in the role-dialogue here, brushes aside Aunt Fact's leveling, he is being insensitive to her needs. Notice that when Aunt Fact offers to compromise it takes some of the steam out of Hunch's aggressiveness. Watch for times when one player is trying hard to think of compromises that will bring about a solution and his opponent is not trying at all.

If both players are stubborn and the roleplay gets bogged down, stop the playing and ask the audience if they can see what has happened. Ask them if they can suggest what might be done. If no answer is forthcoming, you might have to suggest that there is some way both could be happy. You may have to model to show them.

Discussion Following the Roleplay. Discussion is always necessary after role-playing. It becomes more important if the players don't try to compromise. Players and audience should be helped to realize that true dialogue is a free exchange of ideas and that, if dialogue is to go on, participants must accept new viewpoints. Barriers must somehow be surmounted. The players should understand that they are looking at a situation from different angles, and each should see that both his viewpoint and that of his opponent may be only partially right.

Discuss "intuitiveness." This is a gut-level feeling of knowing something but not how. If there were instances of good leveling and non-leveling, bring these up so that the players and the audience can realize the difference it makes. Was there any outstanding manipulation? Were there put-downs when a player was being aggressive or defensive? The role-dialogue here shows Aunt Fact using sarcasm for a put-down when she is on the defensive and it gets a negative result. If there have been any instances of negative results from put-downs by either player, discuss them.

THINKING vs FEELING[7]

Explanation of Functions:

THINKING: The Thinking Function tells you "what" a thing is. Miss Hair will take this role. She attacks all problems logically, identifying everything in a precise way. Because she is afraid she cannot control her emotions, she severely represses them. She analyzes facts and has the need to mold or synthesize them into some kind of a pattern or idea. She is the reasoner; logic is her god.

FEELING: Feeling tells you what a thing is "worth" to you. That part is played by Mr. Cool Cat. His feelings are rational and he has them under control at all times. Understanding people and what they want, he uses this tactfully to gain what he feels is right. He is a people's person. Judgment of value is his "thing."

Roleplay 7 (the above Functions personified in a situation):

*Mr. Cool Cat: Hippie sort of character who teaches art at the Hilldale High School. He has used his keen knowledge of humanity to sway many of his co-workers into a teachers' strike for higher pay. He feels values in our society have gone out of kilter. He welcomes the chance to bring to the notice of the community the fact that plumbers are paid more than the teachers of their children.

Miss Hair: Miss Hair is the high school math teacher in this small town. She feels strikes hurt not only the children but also the capacity of the teachers to control and teach. How can you teach your pupils to talk out their problems in an orderly way when you yourself are striking rather than trying to negotiate?

(No dialogue is given with the roleplay; for a guideline, the conductor can use the dialogue to the Open-End Play, which is found after the roleplay suggestions.)

*Role-descriptions are for the conductor only.

Suggestions for the Personification Roleplay "Thinking *vs* Feeling"

Selecting Your Players. How you select players will determine the ease with which this role is played, for it is one of the more difficult roles. If you are acquainted with your audience, you may wish to select the people you feel can best identify with the parts. If you don't know your audience well, read the explanations of the Functions (thinking and feeling) and ask for volunteers who can identify with each part. You should explain that the roles given here show the extreme of the Functions. The ability of your players should be fairly even although in interpersonal relations a person who closely fits the "Feeling" description usually has a slight edge. If you think one of your players is over-matched, pep-talk him or her into greater fighting power.

Instructions for Players. You will be trying to heighten the conflict between the players, so sympathize as much as you can with the player you are addressing and the role he is to play. To Mr. Cool Cat you could say: "You realize Watergates and useless wars will continue until people get their sense of values into clearer focus. What's the matter with some teachers—can't they see that the issue here is more than salaries? Like Miss Hair! She's too rigid. Maybe you can help her open up and live a little!" Etc., etc. To Miss Hair you could say: "Don't these striking teachers realize what they're doing to the children? With the emotions of the whole town aroused, violence could break out at any time! Especially if new teachers are brought in as strike-breakers." Etc.

Don't forget to bring your players into the scene with something immediate. To the Cool Cat player you could say: "Well, well, here comes Miss Hair, the oh-so-proper math teacher. You wonder if she's going to join the strike. That would be news! You go over to greet her." Etc. To the Miss Hair player you could say: "There's Mr. Cool Cat. He's magnetic, all right—personable, attractive, really quite likable. But he's also the leader of this terrible strike. Maybe you can help him see the dangers he's leading the teachers into. It looks like he's coming over to greet you." Etc.

What to Watch for. The aim of the roleplay is understanding the opponent's viewpoint. Watch how the players approach this. The dialogue of the Open-End Play (provided to help the conductor but not the roleplayer) shows something of how these two types of people think and react. The roleplayers may or may not bring this out, depending on how much they use the Function. Watch to see if they stick to their roles and bring this out during discussion. Watch for leveling. If there is leveling the roleplay will move faster and each player will have an easier time understanding his opponent's view. Take notice of when a player is not leveling. Notice when a player can concede a point (as Cool Cat does in the dialogue) and commend the player during the discussion period. Take note of the player who is willing to apologize when wrong (as Miss Hair does about the reason teachers stay in this town). Watch for put-downs that slow the roleplay.

Notice when different types of manipulation are taking place. Both the manipulator and the manipulated may be unaware of this.

Discussion Following the Roleplay. Discussion is especially important with these personifying roles, because the players must be made aware that each of them is simply using a different approach. They should realize that each approach is a valid way of looking at a problem. If both players can understand that each is simply using his or her own best way, they may not spend so much time trying to change their opponent—not only in the roleplay but in their everyday personal relations. If a player has not been able to stick with his role, he may be using his opponent's approach (or another one) in his everyday life rather than the one for the role he has been trying. This is not always easy to see until it is tried.

The game "Who Is Me?" (p. 58) makes use of the Functions (Sensation, Intuition, Thinking, Feeling) and Types (Introvert, Extrovert) described in this chapter and can be played either before or after the roleplays. The game can be used to give everyone—both roleplayers and audience—a chance to determine which Function and Type he or she feels most at ease with.

If there has been manipulation among your players, you might like to have them look at another way of reacting (see "Contrasting as a Discussion Technique," p. 70). If there is enough interest, your group may want to play the manipulation game on page 63.

THINKING *vs* FEELING

Open-End Play:

(Open-End Plays are not roleplays but simply short skits that make no attempt at an ending. After play-reading this skit you can discuss possible endings, but that isn't necessary. The objective of an Open-End Play is to provide a medium for discussion. In this skit the interaction between the two Functions, Thinking and Feeling, is shown to bring out points necessary for understanding and discussion. If for some reason both the roleplay and the Open-End Play are needed, use the roleplay first so as not to inhibit the creativity of the roleplayers.)

[Scene: Strikers are demonstrating in front of the Hilldale High School in a small town in Wisconsin. Mr. Cool Cat, who is among them, sees Miss Hair walking toward the group. Knowing her feelings about strikes, he wonders what she is doing here. He goes forward to greet her.]

Cool Cat: Well, Miss Hair, have you come to join our little strike?

Miss Hair: Surely you know better than that! I'm hoping to convince some of these teachers of the falsity of their thinking.

Cool Cat: Are you sure it's thinking that persuades them to be a part of this agitation? Couldn't it be an instinctive feeling for what is right and worthwhile? Why bring thinking into the picture?

Miss Hair: My dear Mr. Cool Cat, thinking is responsible for the technological miracles of our civilization. Why go back to the cave age?

Cool Cat: You mean it's better to kill a man with an atomic bomb or flame-thrower than to just hit him over the head?

Miss Hair: No, of course not. But what has that got to do with this strike?

Cool Cat: Our civilization amounts to nothing without a clearer picture of what is worthwhile and what isn't. Here in our own bailiwick, it's higher wages for teachers. We somehow must get the school board to listen to our pleas.

Miss Hair: But didn't most of the teachers come to this small town because they were inexperienced and probably couldn't command the salary of a larger school?

Cool Cat: Speak for yourself, Miss Hair. Many of the teachers, including me, are here because this is our home.

Miss Hair: I'm sorry—I didn't know that. But if salary is so important, couldn't you go where you would get higher wages?

Cool Cat: Yes, we could. But we like this town. To me, teaching is more important than plumbing. But here plumbers are paid considerably more than teachers are. Low salaries do not encourage the best caliber of teachers.

Miss Hair: But is disruption the best way to help? Have you thought this over carefully enough?

Cool Cat: You bet we have! Everyone involved in this strike risks not only his job here but rehiring in the profession.

Miss Hair: I know! So why risk it?

Cool Cat: This technological age you talk about has advanced without a decent sense of values. There isn't enough emphasis on what is really worthwhile. Someone has got to take risks to make this town aware of what it's doing.

Miss Hair: But the risk you're taking is too great! And is it really good for the children?

Cool Cat: I sincerely believe it is. Our children should be made aware of the lopsided sense of values. They should be encouraged to take risks for what they can see is right.

Miss Hair: But that's just the point! Will the children see the issue or only notice your methods?

Cool Cat: What do you mean?

Miss Hair: What if some of these children become plumbers and remember the strike only as a means of getting higher pay? Won't that undo what you hope to achieve?

Cool Cat: You have a point there. They should be made aware of the real issue!

Miss Hair: Wouldn't it be better just to arbitrate?

Cool Cat: Arbitration is failing, Miss Hair. We need action!

Miss Hair: But strikes arouse negative emotions. Already people are talking about replacing the striking teachers. There could even be violence!

WHO IS ME?

Game 3

AIM OF THE GAME: To help players get acquainted.

To help players become aware that their friends and associates may approach problems from a different angle. Implies people are unique.

PLAYERS: If the group is large it would be best to break into groups of from 4 to 6 players. A group leader, who has had some briefing, should then be provided for each group.

MATERIALS: Blackboard or easel. Photocopies of the explanations of Types and Functions found on pp. 46, 49, and 53. Photocopies of the descriptions of Superior Functions in text of game, and photocopies of the Function Wheel.

This is a game for Carl Jung buffs. Carl Jung believed that because of unique conditions, from childhood on we tend to become more and more comfortable and more and more skilled in approaching a problem in a certain way.[8] This is done subconsciously and often we are unaware of how we approach things.

Young people are often upset when an admired parent, an older brother or sister, or even peers ask questions like: "Why have you always got your head stuck in a book?" "Why are you always going off half-cocked? Can't you lay out the facts first?" Young people are not always aware of why they approach a problem the way they do. They do know that when they try to do the things the way their parents or peers advise, they sometimes become confused. Young people must be helped to realize that perhaps their own way *is* best. They may be unconsciously following the pathway of a Function or Type and no one way is any better than the other. Each is a valid way of adjusting to life. Moreover, the way they have unconsciously picked has proved the best way for them. It is wise to avoid an extreme in any direction, but each person is unique and must be allowed to be himself or herself. They should be proud of saying, "I gotta be me!" But who is me?

Part 1. It would be best to start with the Types, *Extrovert* and *Introvert*. The group leader should have an assistant read the Type descriptions from the photocopied explanation of Types while he jots down the points for all to see on a blackboard. He will explain to the group that all will have some characteristics of both but a tendency toward one more than the other. If this is to be used as a get-acquainted game, the leader will give his name, and some facts about himself, then mention the Type he thinks he might be.

If he chooses Introvert, he might like to tell this story: (Extrovert could tell the story from his own point of view) My older brother, who is now a successful salesman, took an occupational test that asked the question: If you had your choice of reading a good book or going to a party which would you choose? My brother thought it a silly question—naturally everyone would want to go to the party! My brother was an Extrovert, always asking me, "Why do you always have your head stuck in a book?" Well, I now have confidence enough in myself to answer, "For the same reason you always like to be with a group of people. We're different!"

The group leader should then allow each one in his group to follow his example of giving his name, some facts about himself, and his Type. They may want to stop here, or go on with the Functions.

Part 2. A. The Functions are more difficult but well worth the effort. The leader should start by drawing a circle and putting in the four Functions, pointing out their relative positions. He will then draw another circle and put in just one Function. Suppose the group leader uses *Thinking* as his Superior Function; it's the Function he uses the most and so easily that he's almost unaware of using it. On the upper quarter of the circle the leader will write "Thinking." As his assistant reads the explanation of the Function from the photocopy, he will jot down descriptive words. He could explain his own experiences with this particular Function or use the example (or have his assistant read the example) provided below:

"I attack a problem by first figuring out just precisely what the problem is and then reason it out in a logical way. I sort out available data; then I analyze and synthesize it."

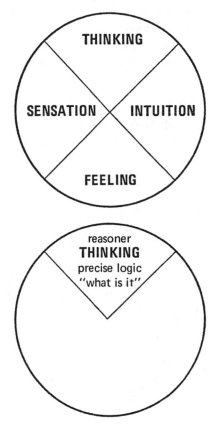

59

B. The group leader should then take the opposite Function on the wheel, which in this case is *Feeling*, drawing the circle and putting in the descriptive words as they are given. He should explain that for HIM as a Thinking Type this is his Inferior Function because he uses it so seldom. After all you can't be feeling something and reasoning it out at the same time! Knowing that he represses the Feeling Function has helped him to realize that Thinking, the opposite on the Function Wheel, was his Superior Function. Although he represses the Function, he knows his sister uses the Feeling Function as her Superior Function.

"This sister of mine seems to know me better than I know myself, and everyone else for that matter! She doesn't bother to think out a problem; just deals with the people involved. She bases her judgments on worth, evaluating things by emotionally toned experiences: I feel this is good, but that is bad. I feel this is morally right; that is morally wrong.[9] She twists the whole family around her little finger, but she's nice to have around when you need some understanding."

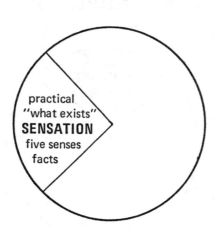

C. The group leader will then go to either side of his Superior Function on the wheel for a Primary Auxiliary Function, depending on which of these two Functions he uses more. He can use both of these as auxiliaries, but here again he will tend to use one more than the other since he can't be perceiving shadowy possibilities at the same time he is perceiving the concreteness of things. If he selects *Sensation*, he will again draw a circle and jot down the descriptive terms. He will explain that this is HIS Primary Auxiliary Function, for, next to Thinking, he uses it the most. But his brother Harry uses the Sensation Function as his Superior Function.

"Harry perceives things as they are by what he can observe with his five senses. He knows things exist when he can see them. He is concerned only with facts, and the strength and pleasure of the sensation. He is painfully practical, concentrating on plain solid sense. And he really gets upset when a project takes an unexpected turn he can't understand! He claims he's a 'hedonist' and seems proud of it.[10] And he can sometimes have all the details of an event, yet miss the general all over picture.[11] "

D. The group leader will then go to the last Function, in this case the *Intuitive* Function. He draws the circle and puts in the terms when they are given. He thinks of his friend Hub when this Function is mentioned.

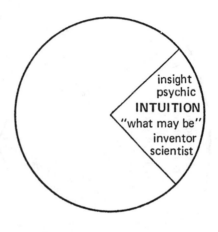

"When I ask Hub how he deals with a problem, I don't think he knows how he does it. He just plays a hunch and goes on from there. He seems to know the gist of the matter in an abstract way, and doesn't seem to be concerned with details or arriving at any reasonable conclusion or judgment. What makes it so hard to understand is that he is so often right—without taking the trouble to figure it out! That tends to bug me! He tells me he's going in for quantum physics. They're welcome to each other!"

Often it is hard to choose the Superior Function from between two Functions. If the player can figure out the Function he uses the least or represses, his Superior Function will be the opposite to this on the Function Wheel. This wheel can be found on the following page. The wheel also helps the player in determining his Function by showing him the types of people that combine the Functions (the in-between area) and the types of people that introvert and extrovert the Functions.

The Function Wheel [12]

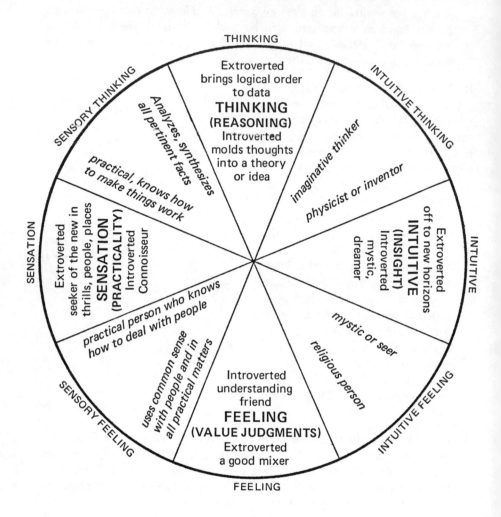

MANIPULATIVE BASKETBALL

Game 4

AIM: To gain an awareness of manipulation.

Everett Shostrom, author of the book, *Man, the Manipulator*, believes it is not necessary to reject manipulations—only to be aware of them—increasing awareness leads naturally to *actualization*.[13] He describes the term *actualizing* as creative behavior (Thou-thou) in contrast to the self-defeating behavior (It-it) of the person who manipulates.[14]

PLAYERS: Eleven players (five for each team) and a Referee
Four Forwards (2 on a team)—"Top-Dog" manipulators
Four Guards (2 on a team)—"Under-Dog" manipulators
Two Centers (1 on a team)—each "Taps" ball for his team
One Referee played by the conductor

The Center—The Center is the hardest position on the team and should be given to the best and sharpest players. The two Centers should be of equal fighting ability (or as near as possible). They will not only have to be well acquainted with the game, but know each player's Primary Manipulation and his opposite polarity.

Forwards and Guards—Each of these players will have to figure out his own primary manipulative pattern and choose this position on the team if possible. Try to have all eight types represented (they are listed below). But in any case, all types on one team must be different. Have two "Top-Dog" and two "Under-Dog" manipulators on each team; these will be the Forwards and Guards respectively. To help these players choose their positions and play them, Shostrom's types are listed below. The wheel on the following page will show "Top-Dog and "Under-Dog" positions and also the polarity of the type. Each player should know the polarity of his type; he will use this as his Reversal Role in the game. The actualizations of each manipulative position are also shown, with people who exemplify them.

Shostrom's Manipulative Types:[15]*

1. *The Dictator* exaggerates his strength. He dominates, orders, quotes authorities, and does anything that will control his victims. Variations of the Dictator are the Mother Superiors, Father Superiors, the Rank-Pullers, the Boss, the Junior Gods.

*From MAN, THE MANIPULATOR by Everett Shostrom. Copyright © 1967 by Abingdon Press. Used by permission.

2. *The Weakling* is usually the Dictator's victim, his polar opposite. The Weakling develops great skill in coping with the Dictator. He exaggerates his sensitivity. He forgets, doesn't hear, is passively silent. Variations of the Weakling are the Worrier, the "Stupid-Like-a Fox," the Giver-Upper, the Confused, the Withdrawer.

3. *The Calculator* exaggerates his control. He deceives, lies, and constantly tries to outwit and control other people. Variations of the Calculator are the High-Pressure Salesman, the Seducer, the Poker Player, the Con Artist, the Blackmailer, the Intellectualizer.

4. *The Clinging Vine* is the polar opposite of the Calculator. He exaggerates his dependency. He is the person who wants to be led, fooled, taken care of. He lets others do his work for him. Variations of the Clinging Vine are the Parasite, the Crier, the Perpetual Child, the Hypochondriac, the Attention Demander, the Helpless One.

5. *The Bully* exaggerates his aggression, cruelty, and unkindness. He controls by implied threats of some kind. He is the Humiliator, the Hater, the Tough Guy, the Threatener. The female variation is the Bitch or Nagger.

6. *The Nice Guy* exaggerates his caring, love, and kills with kindness. In one sense, he is much harder to cope with than the Bully. You can't fight a Nice Guy! Curiously, in a conflict with the Bully, Nice Guy almost always wins! Variations of the Nice Guy are the Pleaser, the Nonviolent One, the Nonoffender, the Noninvolved One, the Virtuous One, the Never-Ask-for-What-You-Want One, the Organization Man.

7. *The Judge* exaggerates his criticalness. He distrusts everybody and is blameful, resentful, slow to forgive. Variations of the Judge are the Know-It-All, the Blamer, the Deacon, the Resentment Collector, the Should-er, the Shamer, the Comparer, the Vindicator, the Convictor.

8. *The Protector* is the opposite of the Judge. He exaggerates his support and is nonjudgmental to a fault. He spoils others, is oversympathetic, and refuses to allow those he protects to stand up and grow up for themselves. Instead of caring for his own needs, he cares only for others' needs. Variations of the Protector are the Mother Hen, the Defender, the Embarrased-for-Others, the Fearful-for-Others, the Sufferer-for-Others, the Martyr, the Helper, the Unselfish One.

Preparation:

As in ordinary basketball, for this game you need to spend some time on skills and warming up sessions before you actually play.

Free Throw Practice—Have your players form a circle around the Referee-conductor. After giving an example of the Ball-Word, the Referee will explain what the Ball-Statement is and give an example to go with the Ball-Word.

The Shostrom Wheel [16*]

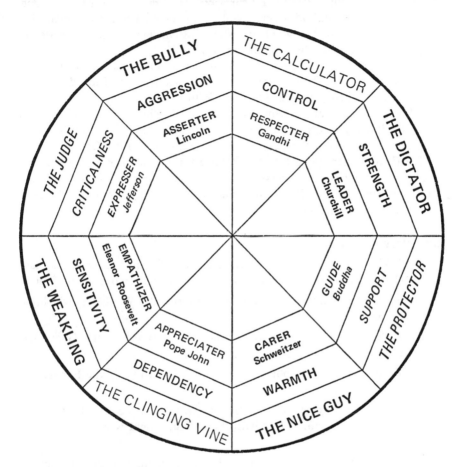

If anyone in the circle would like to try a Ball-Statement have him do so. If not, take the example and go around the circle, having each player give a manipulative reply from the easiest position (usually the Weakling or Bully). You may need a few examples to get started. For practicing (after the idea catches on), you could use a real basketball to throw to the player you want a reply from.

Center Skills—The people who will be the Centers should be given the chance to read over all the material, trying it out on their own until they get the feel of it. Until the group catches on to the game, the adult advisers might take the Center positions.

*From MAN, THE MANIPULATOR by Everett Shostrom. Copyright © 1967 by Abingdon Press. Used by permission.

Play Action of the Game:

Referee tosses up the "Ball-Word"—the word or phrase that starts the game. After hearing the word, both Centers will try to come up with a statement that is somehow related to the word and that will challenge their teammates to manipulate. This is called the "Ball-Statement."

The first Center to translate the Ball-Word into a Ball-Statement for one of his teammates wins the Toss. This Center is then said to have "Tapped the Ball" and the game is then played in his court. With the Ball-Statement this Center must also clearly call out the name of the teammate who is to respond, and if it is to be his Primary or his Reversal Role. If the designated teammate is able to respond correctly, then the team is given four points for a "Field Goal."

The Centers then go back to the Referee for another Toss-Up. When each player on one team has had a chance to respond with both his Primary Role and its opposite (his Reversal Role), the game will be declared over and the team with the most points is declared the winner.

Terminology and Rules:

Ball-Word—Word or phrase that the Referee gives out for the Centers to translate into Ball-Statements. The Ball-Word is heard by everyone in the game.

Ball-Statement—A statement loosely related to the Ball-Word that will bring forth a manipulative reply.

Primary Role—The manipulation that either the Forward or the Guard has chosen to play.

Reversal Role—The opposite polarity of the manipulative role the Forward or Guard has chosen to play.

Toss-Up—When the Referee calls out the Ball-Word, this is called the Toss-Up. The Center who responds first with the Ball-Statement is said to have won the Toss.

Tapping-the-Ball—When one Center gets the jump on his opponent by getting his statement in first, he Taps the Ball and the game is then played in his court.

Field Goal—When a Forward or Guard has successfully responded to the Ball-Statement, he has made a Field Goal which is good for *four points*.

Time! (referee)—Referee may call Time when he is undecided about any Ball-Statement or manipulative answer. He may get help from any of the players by questions. He will depend on each Center to defend his team's interests, and will let a good try go by unless the other Center objects.

Time! (center)—Center may also ask for Time, for he is the defender of his team. The Referee has many rules to remember and will depend on each

Center to be vigilant for his team's best interests. The Center will, however, only be alerting the Referee to a possible infringement. The Referee makes the final decision.

Free Throw—A chance for the opposing team to complete a Ball-Statement. Points received correspond to the points given for the Foul.

Fouls—Called when the Ball-Statement isn't brought home or if there is some infraction of the rules.

Two-Point Foul—This Foul is called when the Ball-Statement is not given a response. Sometimes the Center's statement is too far afield for the team-mate to rescue; sometimes the player may just not have a response. After a player gives up or a reasonable time elapses, a Foul is declared and a two-point Free Throw given. Any player on the opposing team can take this incompleted Ball-Statement and use his Primary Role to respond. If his reply is successful, his team will receive *TWO POINTS*.

One-Point Foul—(1) This Foul is used when one Center is repeatedly jumping in unprepared, i.e. with a Ball-Statement that is not related to the Ball-Word. If Time is called and the Center himself is unable to show the connection, the opposing Center is given a one-point Free Throw to attempt to change the offending Ball-Statement to comply with the rules. If the Referee decides he has succeeded, *one point* is awarded.

(2) The Center has a great deal of material to keep in his head and this is part of the game. If he forgets and calls for a Role that his teammate has already responded with, a Foul is called with a one-point Free Throw. A Forward on the opposing team may take the offending Ball-Statement and respond to it if he can, using his Primary Role. If he is successful, his team receives *ONE POINT*.

(3) If a Forward or a Guard uses an incorrect response or mixes his Primary and Reversal roles, he receives a Foul with a one-point Free Throw for the opposing team. A corresponding Forward or Guard on the opposing team may take the same Ball-Statement and try to answer it, using his Primary Role. If he is successful, his team receives *ONE POINT*.

Examples of the Play Action:

BALL-WORD: *Abortion.*

The Ball-Statement might be: "I'm going to have a baby!" The center will then call out the name of the player he wants to respond and which role he wants him or her to use. Example: Jack :: Protector.

Protector: "I don't care who's responsible, dear. I'll stand by. I can't bear the thought of your having an abortion. We'll get married. School and my career aren't important."

Other players could react to the same Ball-Statement:

Dictator: "It's about time someone took you in hand. I'll arrange for an abortion. I have influence."

Weakling: "Oh my goodness! What will you do? Have you been thinking of an abortion? This is too much for me. I'll worry myself into the grave!"

Calculator: "No big deal. Get an abortion. This would make interesting news to a few people I know!"

Clinging Vine: "What do you expect me to do? Oh dear, I'm not feeling well. I'm getting such a headache."

Bully: "Don't expect me to pay for any abortion. You got yourself into this, you get yourself out. This is just about what I would expect from *you*."

Nice Guy: "Oh you poor kid! I don't like to advise you on anything like this, but I'll help any way I can, you know that!"

Judge: "My dear! How could you do such a thing? Aren't you ashamed of yourself? An abortion may be needed."

A Ball-Statement like "I'm pregnant and you're responsible!" would be more directed to the Bully who could respond: "Why you silly dope, I was only one of a half dozen other guys! Don't try using my name, or you'll be sorry! Don't expect me to pay for an abortion!" Etc.

BALL-WORD: *Watergate.*

Teammates should help the Center "bring in" the Ball-Statement no matter how preposterous it seems. So if the Ball-Statement is: "The moon is made of green cheese," the Calculator as an intellectualizer could cite the moon expeditions and accuse him of lying to the uninformed; the weakling could just play dumb and withdraw by saying: "Oh, are you sure? I'm always puzzled by these things."

BALL-WORD: *Cheating.*

1. Ball-Statement: "Here is my exam paper, Teacher."
   Center to Forward: "Sally :: Dictator."
   The Mother Superior in the Dictator could respond: I hope it's all your own work, Bill. We must be careful to be honest if we hope to succeed in life."

2. Ball-Statement: "My three aces win the pot. Anyone want to make something of that?"
   a. Center to Guard: "George :: Weakling."
   The Giver-Upper with a touch of Stupid-Like-a-Fox: "No, of course not. I guess I'm just stupid. I was trying for aces, too."
   b. Center to Guard: "Harry :: Clinging Vine."
   Bringing out the Crier, the helpless One: "Oh, I'm wiped out. What will I do? Could you possibly spare some of the money for my children?"

3. Ball-Statement: "I'm going to be busy at work tonight so I won't be able to keep our date."
Center to Guard: "Debbie :: Clinging Vine."
Bringing out the Parasite in the Clinging Vine: "Oh, I had *so* counted on your being with me tonight. I get so lonesome sometimes I think I'll end it all."

Clarification of Rules and Helpful Hints

1. Exaggerate manipulations so there can be no question of their passing. Manipulation is the aim of the game.

2. Because everyone has heard the Ball-Word, it is not necessary for the Ball-Statement to make it clear. With the Ball-Word in mind the player should be trying to respond to what the Center has given in any way he can.

3. Centers are allowed some leniency. If a Center forgets the Primary or Reversal Role of a player, he can just call out the player's name with "Primary" or "Reversal," hoping his teammate can use it with his statement.

4. Ball-Words and Ball-Statements can imply different things and can be used in different ways. A teammate may use the Ball-Statement in a manner completely different from what the Center had in mind. It would still be correct.

5. It is not necessary to mention the Ball-Word in the manipulative answer to the Ball-Statement. But encourage the players to do so where they can, since it helps clarify their reasoning.

6. Forwards and Guards should take note: If you make no attempt to answer a Ball-Statement, the opposing team gets TWO points and any member of the opposing team can try to reply. This is a stiff penalty! It is a great deal stiffer than having your try judged a wrong response and losing only ONE point. Moreover, if the Referee feels it is a good try, he may say nothing. If the opposing Center does not object, it will get by. The game is structured to encourage trying.

7. Remember, the main purpose of the game is to get the Forwards and Guards to manipulate. If you are having a hard time getting anyone to fill the Center spots (because they are difficult), subsidize this position by allowing the Centers to see the full list from which you will be choosing the Ball-Word. In this way they can prepare a general Ball-Statement for each of the words. If using Primary and Reversal Roles makes it too tough at first, use only Primary Roles.

Suggested Ball-Words:

Watergate	Lying	Illness	Love
Open Marriage	Cheating	Blackmail	Sex
Threatening	Abortion	Comparison	Women's Liberation
Jealousy	Siblings	Prejudice	

Contrasting as a Discussion Technique for Manipulation[17]

THE MANIPULATOR (It-It Relationship)	THE ACTUALIZOR (Thou-Thou Relationship)
Deception (Phoniness, Knavery) a) Uses tricks, techniques. b) Plays a role only to create a desired impression. Puts on an act to maneuver his antagonist.	**Honesty** (Genuineness, Authenticity) a) Is able to be himself, whatever it may be. b) Expresses himself the way he is feeling it. Is candid and genuine; always leveling.
Unawareness (Deadness, Boredom) a) Has "tunnel vision," seeing and hearing only what he wishes to. b) Unaware of the really important concerns of living. c) Sees life as a battle. d) Feels unappreciated and unvaluable, regards others the same way (as "its").	**Awareness** (Responsiveness, Aliveness, Interest) a) Looks at and listens to himself and others. b) Fully aware of all the dimensions of living. c) Sees life as a growth process. d) Appreciates all aspects of himself and others.
Control (Closed, Deliberate) a) Regards life as a game of chess; calculates every move. b) Concealing his motives, he controls himself and others. c) Demands or is submissive. d) Chooses to control others.	**Freedom** (Spontaneity, Openness) a) Is spontaneous. b) Allows himself and others freedom to express potentials. c) Not a puppet or an object, but master of his life. d) Chooses to contact others.
Cynicism (Distrust) a) Distrusts himself and others; doesn't trust human nature.	**Trust** (Faith, Belief) a) Has deep trust in himself and others, and can cope with life in the here and now.

(Discussion with Contrasting is different from other Listings. Here you are trying to coax the meaning of "actualizor" from your participants. They will tend to remember the meaning better if they have thought it through on their own. Ask your players if they can name a trait of manipulators. When they have come up with one, write it on the blackboard, and then ask them to name the opposite trait, which you can write under *Actualizor*. Then ask them to define these traits; and write the opposing definitions under each. Proceed with traits and definitions one by one, letting your *players* do the thinking.)

Suggested reading:
Maria F. Mahoney, *The Meaning in Dreams and Dreaming* (New York: Citadel Press, 1966);
P. W. Martin, *Experiment in Depth* (Boston: Routledge & Kegan Paul, 1976);
Everett L. Shostrom, *Man, the Manipulator* (Nashville: Abingdon Press, 1967).

5

search for identity

A teenager with his fertile mind is like a block of clay waiting to be molded into a figure. The rough outline is there but more work is needed to determine what the figure will be. In understanding himself or herself (an essential part in the search for identity), a youth is taking this lump of clay and is starting to bring out a figure. The last chapter was designed to help each youth realize that he or she is a unique person, and take pride in this, in order to establish an invulnerable core as an individual. In this chapter, youths will go beyond finding out what they are and find out what they can become.

The emerging figure needs to become more distinct. How can the "givens" of the youth, his or her talents, abilities, and interests, be used? They are an important part of this figure. In all things, *mind is the builder*. Any youth can create his or her own path. With aims and goals in mind, the youth can bring about an exciting and fulfilling life. The desire and will of the individual will change these aims many times during a life time, but each time they will have an important part—in molding the clay.

THE BUILDING OF AN EGO

Roleplay 8   (disruptive type of role)

*Jocko: (*Trickster*—loves to play tricks) A person who loves to shock people and play tricks on them. He has found he gets attention this way, and at his stage of development he seems to need it. The conductor will encourage him to interrupt whenever anything constructive is going on. Usually when this is carried to the extreme it will get under the skin of the rest and they will register strong disapproval.

Harvey: (*Hare*—carries flag for a cause) He is easily "turned on" by a cause. An excellent salesman, he has sold most of the tickets for a raffle to send representatives to the Scout Jamboree. The conductor will encourage him to gain the support of his fellow Explorers for his cause.

Horner: (*Red Horn*—champion of the underdog) He seems to get a lift from helping his brother who is down. The conductor will advise him to defend Jocko but not until some disapproval is shown by the others. He will then laugh at Jocko's jokes and interruptions and identify with him.

Mat: (*Twins*—mature hero) He combines the forceful leadership of the extrovert with the considerate understanding of the introvert. The conductor should apprise him of the whole situation and what is being attempted. Mat may have to start the disapproval of Jocko's actions if no one else does. If the role gets too disruptive Mat may have to try to bring order out of chaos.

[The scene opens as Mat comes into the meeting room of the Explorers. Jocko has been tripping everyone as they come in the door. Mat has just managed to keep his footing.]

Mat: Cut it out, Jocko! Your attention everybody. Our leader won't be here until later and he's asked me to take charge. We might as well get started with old business.

Harvey: How about ticket selling for the Scout Jamboree? We're way behind our goal. I've got an idea that might help . . . .

Jocko: Well, what d'you know. The man has an idea.

Harvey: I've thought of something to make selling more fun . . . .

Jocko: Fun man, I'm all for it!

---

*Role-descriptions and dialogue are for the conductor only; they are given as guides.

Suggestions for the Roleplay "The Building of an Ego"

Selecting Your Players. Careful selection of players is necessary for this role. Try to select players who will feel comfortable in their roles and who will enjoy playing them. The players will be portraying the four stages of ego development of the Winnebago Indians.[1] Fighting ability is not as important here as identification with the role.

Instructing Your Players. In this role you will be attempting a *disruptive* type of roleplaying, so give specific advice about it to each of your players, individually, in front of your audience. The stages of ego development mentioned are only for the conductor. Avoid using titles, especially Trickster or Hero.

In giving your instructions, try to instill confidence in each player for his particular role at the same time that you are intensifying the conflict. To Jocko you might say something like: "Things are really dull around these Explorers' meetings and it's up to you to put a little life into them. You can't let them get too serious and turn into another school room! You can always find a trick or gag to pull whenever things are slow. Horner is a friend and likes a good time. Maybe he'd like to help?" And to bring him into the scene: "You're at the weekly Explorer meeting and ole sober-sides Mat has just walked in. How quick is this guy on his feet?"

To Harvey you might say: "The big raffle drawing to get money for delegates to the Scout Jamboree is only about a week away and there aren't nearly enough tickets sold. How can you get the guys into the mood for selling more? Will the prize your father offered (under pressure it's true!) stimulate them enough or will you need something more?" To make Harvey a part of the scene: "You've just gotten to the meeting and been told by one of the guys that the adviser won't be here until later. Mat will be in charge. Will he be able to help you? Will that silly ass Jocko disrupt the meeting again so that you can't get anything done?"

To Horner you could give something like: "You hope the fellows don't pick on Jocko again tonight. Jocko is a great guy, and just likes a little fun once in a while. Things would get really dull without him around." Etc. And to bring him into the scene: "You can see by the merry look in Jocko's eyes that he's in fine form tonight. You wonder where the adviser is. Will Mat know?"

To Mat you might say: "Your role will be essentially a prop role; it will be up to you to keep things rolling, and prevent chaos. You will handle Jocko's tricks in as mature a way as you can. If the others don't object to his tricks and interruptions, you may have to instigate some objections and curb him—getting the others to follow you. You will help Harvey in promoting the ticket sale, but wait for him to take the initiative." To plunge Mat into the scene, say something like: "You have just arrived at the Explorers' meeting and will have to get it started, since the adviser won't be here until later. Will you be able to manage the guys?"

What to Watch for. Watch to see how Jocko manages his role. Are his tricks subtle and a certain amount of fun, or are they crude and obnoxious? If they are crude, do the other players object, speaking out in a candid way, or do they hold their feelings inside in resentment? Does this resentment come out in put-downs and sarcasm? Or if the other players are enjoying Jocko, do they object to Mat's trying to stop him? Each way will present a problem for someone to work out.

Watch to see how Harvey gets the attention of the other players. How successful is he in interesting them in the sales competition? Does he persuade smoothly or in a haranguing manner? Has he made his cause their cause? Is he able to take Jocko's interruptions in stride?"

Take notice of how Horner helps Jocko. Does he help the other players enjoy the fun of "goofing off," or does he seem to be just another Jocko making everyone uncomfortable?

The role of Mat is a prop role, but how does the player handle it? Can he fend off Jocko's tricks and interruptions in a firm way but not belabor them? Does he manage to keep things rolling? If Jocko is popular, is Mat able to gain the support of his fellow Explorers in trying to stop Jocko? Has he been able to help Harvey interest the others in ticket selling? Does leveling or manipulation play a big part during the roleplaying?

Discussion Following the Roleplay. Explain to the Jocko-player that rejection of his tricks was part of the role. Find out how he was feeling during the playing. Ask the audience if they can see any parallel between the Jocko character and the Br'er Rabbit stories. Discuss any connection they might see between the part of Jocko and frustrated rioters' breaking windows and destroying things. How does Jocko compare with the natural child of the PAC concept of Berne and Harris (pp. 20, 98)? Discuss clowns, jesters, and comedians, who with exaggerations help us look at ourselves and laugh at our own imperfections. Bring out in the discussion how the natural child adds spice and fun to living.

How has the Harvey-player handled getting the attention of his fellow players? If he was not too successful ask the other players or the audience if they can think of better ways it might have been done. Ask the audience if they can see any parallel between the Harvey-character and the college students who worked for civil rights and other causes. If the Horner-player has been drawn down to Jocko's level of tricks, try to bring out in discussion how this may have happened. Bring your audience into the discussion by asking how they might have handled the problem.

Unless Mat has been a complete disaster, commend him for playing a difficult part. Have him tell what was the hardest thing he had to do and why. Find out if he was aware of any lack of leveling among the players. Did the Mat-player or any of the others use forms of manipulation?

"What Is Maturity?" as a listing technique (p. 104) can be used to advantage here. The game PAC Pinball (p. 98) is also applicable.

FORCES CRIPPLING THE EGO

Roleplay 9

*Terry: A teenage ADC mother with a baby. Life has dealt Terry one bad deal after another. Her father deserted her and her mother when she was a small child. Rather than get help from the government, her mother decided to work, and this left little time for Terry or housework. Other mothers supplied their daughters with the pill and made sure they took them. But not *her* mother! Her mother told her that if she was just going to lie around she'd have to start earning her *own* money. Then she got pregnant, and, not having the money, she had waited too long to have an abortion. Even then she had thought it would be nice to have a home of her own—and a baby of her very own to love her! But it hadn't turned out that way. Life now had become a drag and she wondered if it was worth living. If she had a lot of money it would change everything.

Gwen: A girl living in the apartment next to Terry's. Having just graduated from high school, she is working this summer to earn money to attend the university in the fall. She will be getting a degree in psychology—she wants to be a social worker. Although not a close friend, Gwen had known Terry in high school before she had her baby. Because Terry has been trying to cling to her in a one-sided friendship, Gwen feels she should jar her into leading a more balanced life.

[Action takes place in Gwen's apartment, in a building in one of the poorer sections of a university town. The scene opens with a knock on Gwen's door; she opens it and there stands Terry, slouching.]

(No dialogue is given here; as a guideline, the conductor can use the dialogue of the Open-End Play [p. 80].)

*Role descriptions are for the conductor only.

Suggestions for the Roleplay "Forces Crippling the Ego"

Selecting Your Players. With this role ask for volunteers. You might ask specific people if they would be willing to play Terry as a prop role. If no one wants to, it might be best to use the Open-End Play. In asking for volunteers to play the ADC mother, you should explain that it is a prop role of a girl who has had a rough deal in life and is depressed and discouraged. You will be trying to give the Gwen-player a foil to work against, but you will also be providing a medium for someone who can identify with the discouraged-girl part (do not make the latter goal too obvious, however). The players' abilities here are not as important as their identification with the roles.

Instructions for Players. Remember, the role-descriptions and dialogue (from the Open-End Play) should not be given to roleplayers; it will inhibit their creativity. Inspire your players for their roles by a confidential one-to-one talk. If you yourself can feel some sympathy for the part, this will carry over in your voice and "body language." To the Terry-player you might say: "Life has sure dealt you a bad hand. Maybe you ought to throw it in—simply pull out of this game. After all, is it worth so much pain? Some people have all the luck; you sure haven't been given any! Your father ran away. Your mother . . . ." Be creative and help your player be free to level about how she is really feeling. Bring her into the scene with something like: "You have just realized you need some groceries if you and the baby are going to eat today. You have absolutely no desire to go out. Maybe Gwen will get some things for you. She is usually pretty good about it. You go and knock on her door."

To the Gwen-player you could try something like: "You're going to try to get a degree in psychology so you can be a social worker. You've wondered what kind of help you will be, and Terry with her baby is an opportunity to find out. She is obviously discouraged and not likely to change with the way she is looking at life. Maybe you can help her." Etc. Bring your player into the role with: "There is a knock on the door. You go to answer it and there stands Terry. This is unusual; she is usually watching TV at this hour."

What to Watch for. Watch for ways the Gwen-player tries to help. Is she so sympathetic that she encourages Terry in her sullen approach to life? Or is she so rough on her that her help comes across as put-downs and makes the girl feel more depressed and bitter? Does the Gwen-player seem like a critical and chastising parent? Are the players leveling so that the action moves forward? Watch for defensiveness and resentment in the Terry-player, or manipulative helplessness. This is one role in which the Terry-player may be prudent to ignore what is uncomfortable for it might indicate a basically different philosophy. Such brushing aside, however, may not help the progress of the role. It should be noted so it can be brought out in the discussion period. Be careful not to condemn a player, who in spite of her real feelings, played the role as written.

Watch for manipulation. This can be from both the Gwen-player and the Terry-player. If a player does try it, how does the other one handle it? With more manipulation?

Discussion Following the Roleplay. If your Terry-player begins to feel anxious or upset, proceed with caution. Discuss the ways the Gwen-player tries to help. Are they effective? Ask the Terry-player how she felt about the help. Can the audience suggest other ways of helping or advice that may have been more effective? Have the audience list the crippling and positive points illustrated by the Open-End Play (as on p. 82). Help bring out these points by asking questions. Center a discussion on the points listed. How are they crippling? How do the positive aims tend to help?

If manipulation was used during the roleplay, bring it out in discussion. The conductor may wish to use the contrasting on manipulation (p. 70) as a discussion technique. If there was a great deal of manipulation, and the group is interested or curious, play the game "Manipulative Basketball" (p. 63). The game "The Royal Order of the Symbol" (p. 92) might also be played after this roleplay to emphasize how positive aims can change the direction in one's life.

FORCES CRIPPLING THE EGO

Open-End Play:

[This is an Open-End Play covering the same material as the above roleplay. The skit, showing the interaction of two people with different philosophies of life, will bring up points helpful to a discussion of a difficult subject. The scene opens as in the roleplay, when Gwen, the girl aspiring to be a social worker, opens her apartment door to find Terry, the teenage ADC mother.]

*Gwen: Come in, Terry, Your TV hasn't broken down, has it?

Terry: No. The news is on now. Martha said she thought you were going grocery shopping this morning.

Gwen: Yes, I planned to go about ten. Would you like to go along?

Terry: Nau. I just thought maybe you would get me a few things?

Gwen: It would do you good to get out, Terry. Keeping your eyes glued to that TV set is demoralizing.

Terry: It's the only decent thing in this crummy world! For a little while I can pretend I'm someone else.

Gwen: But what happens when the program ends and you're you again?

Terry: [shrugs shoulder] There's always another program. [looking around] It really looks nice in here.

Gwen: Your apartment's the same as mine—or was!

Terry: You haven't got holes in your plaster. I told the old landlord about it ages ago but he hasn't done anything. He makes me furious!

Gwen: Is that where your babysitter ran his bike into the wall?

Terry: Yeah. And he's knocked out other pieces since. That damn kid! I pay him to watch the baby so I can sleep and get a little peace. And, you know, sometimes he's more trouble than the baby.

Gwen: Maybe you had better fix the plaster yourself—and clean up the apartment. I have a feeling the landlord will move you out before he does anything there.

Terry: Oh, we'll just get moved into that new building they're putting up.

Gwen: Think you could keep that place up any better?

---

*This Open-End Play is to be used after (or in place of) the roleplay so as not to inhibit the creativity of the roleplayers.

Terry: Gosh, Gwen. [puzzled] I didn't think you would mind my having a nice place to live.

Gwen: I'm sorry, Terry. I'm just trying to show you that moving into a new place isn't the answer to your problem.

Terry: I didn't know I had a problem.

Gwen: I realize that. When you worked in the laundry, Terry, did you ever feel proud of a shirt you had ironed?

Terry: Heck no! I thought of how much I hated it and the big baboon who was our boss.

Gwen: Have you ever wanted to do some special work, like—like maybe fixing hair?

Terry: [walking toward mirror] My hair looks sexy when I fix it, huh? [looks in mirror and makes a face] Well, I haven't had a date in two months.

Gwen: Your hair is beautiful, and especially when it's freshly washed!

[Phone rings in Terry's apartment and she runs offstage to answer it. She can be heard saying 'Oh yes!' in an excited tone. She comes back into the room in a thoughtful manner.]

Terry: That was my friend Mary. She tells me there's a real slick guy looking for a date next Friday. And, well . . .

Gwen: What?

Terry: My place is such a *mess*! I wondered if maybe we could exchange apartments for the evening.

Gwen: So you wouldn't have to clean your own?

Terry: But there's the broken plaster and the spots on the rugs! The baby throws food all over and it gets tracked on the rugs. If I clean it, it'll be a mess in a short time anyway.

Gwen: And it'll continue to be messed until you start cleaning it up when the food spills.

Terry: What about the apartment?

Gwen: The answer is a definite no!

Terry: Hey, you aren't one of those people who are against an ADC mother getting a little sex, are you?

Gwen: No, Terry. In view of the rest of your life it probably looks like a positive element to you. But why not look for something more than sex?

Terry: Nothing wrong with sex, as far as I'm concerned. I don't like to get too involved. Damn guys expect too much. Then when you're hooked they desert you.

Gwen: Not all men are like your father, Terry.

Terry: Says who? Look, let's drop that. How about me fixing your hair? Will you switch then?

Gwen: Nope. Wait. [hesitates] You like fixing hair and you're good at it. I'll make a deal with you.

Terry: What kind of a deal?

Gwen: You fix my hair and clean your apartment, and I'll help you fix it up so you won't be ashamed of it.

Terry: The spots? And the plaster?

Gwen: I'll rent a shampooer, and if all the spots don't come out we'll use an area rug. I've used the plaster they use for drywalls and I can do a passable job. We can get some paint from the landlord. How about it?

Terry: Well . . . . I'll have to think about it.

Listing as a Discussion Technique: Forces Crippling the Ego

[After the Open-End Play the conductor may wish to have the audience list the different elements that are crippling. Then list what could be positive elements.]

*Crippling Forces:	*Positive Forces:
Asking for life as a gift.	Choosing work she likes.
Projecting own faults unto others.	Working with talents she has.
Non-producing.	Producing something creative.
Living against life instead of for it.	Accepting new ideas and trying them.
Retreating from life.	Being proud of something.
Contriving a life of imagery instead of real life.	Making realistic plans or aims for the future.
Using up energy in anger and hatred.	Making meaningful relationships.
Toying with a fairy dream of what she would like to be instead of what she can be.	Not letting fears of the past rob her of new experiences.
Avoiding deep relationships.	
Looking for gratification of feelings and entertainment rather than something deeper.	

*These are only suggestions. Allow your audience the freedom to come up with their own ideas.

FORCES FOR A HEALTHY EGO

Roleplay 10

*Clint: Brilliant high school senior who enjoys schoolwork and is challenged by new ideas—especially in physics. Clint's parents died many years ago and he has been brought up by guardians. They were very impersonal and Clint was often lonely. Now, however, he is on his own with full control of the money his parents left him. Up until now, Clint's inability to relate to people has been unimportant. The lab and his future career as a physicist were all that mattered. But now there is something new—something besides the money. Now there is Nancy!

Nancy: An attractive senior, who is determined to save Clint from the miserable life of being a slave to the establishment. She has seen his need to open up and feel the warmth of human relationships. She dislikes Mr. Paxton, the physics teacher, for he keeps Clint far too busy to have time for social affairs.

Mr. Paxton: High school physics teacher. He sees that Clint has the makings of a brilliant physicist. Aware of Clint's naiveté with girls, he feels Nancy is a danger to Clint's career.

[As the scene opens, Mr. Paxton joins Clint in the physics lab, where Clint has just finished an important experiment.]

Mr. Paxton: How did the experiment come out?

Clint: Great! But I wasn't sure until the end.

Mr. Paxton: You've got a great gift, Clint. You're luckier than most fellows your age. You know what you want to do and you have the ability and the funds to do it. You can go as far as you want to.

Clint: I could wish for a little more experience with girls and more ease with people in general. Nancy has suggested we join a group of her friends at a hippie retreat in California this summer. She claims she'll teach me.

Mr. Paxton: With LSD?

Clint: Come now, Mr. Paxton, I'm not stupid.

Nancy: [coming into the room] Who's not stupid?

---

*Role-descriptions and dialogue are only for the conductor; they are given as guides.

Suggestions for the Roleplay "Forces for a Healthy Ego"

Selecting Your Players. Equal fighting ability would be good here but players' identification with their parts is more important. If you know your audience, select people you know will fight for each particular viewpoint. If not, ask for volunteers.

Instructing Your Players. In this role you will be trying to show how a healthy ego is a balance between positive forces. You should encourage each player to fight for his point of view. It will be up to them to come up with compromises. Try to feel some sympathy for each of the viewpoints; this will carry over when you give your instructions.

To the Clint-player you could say something like: "You have sometimes been lonely without parents or brothers or sisters. Nancy is a new experience—she certainly opens up new vistas of learning—but she also interferes with your work." Etc. And, to bring him into the scene: "You're glad that Nancy is late—you'd never have been able to finish with her there. You want to see her, but later. You're happy to see Mr. Paxton come in the door; you need to talk about the experiment."

To the teacher-player you could say: "You dislike this girl Nancy who is running away from life. She's a bad influence on Clint; except for her he could probably do brilliant things in physics. Clint's parents have left him enough money for whatever education he will need—*if* Nancy doesn't have him throw it away on one of those communes full of freeloaders!" And to bring him in: "Clint's in the lab and you're going to have a talk with him."

To the Nancy-player try something like: "Clint is a real challenge! You have never met anyone so deprived of human relationships. And to top it he's planning a career where he'll be working alone. He needs a job, for a while at least, where he'll have to work with people. You feel a farm or a commune where he'll be able to form new relationships is almost a necessity at his stage in life." Etc. And to plunge her into the scene: "You are late on purpose hoping Clint will be finished with his experiment. He doesn't seem human until he is. You walk into the physics lab, and Clint is there but so is that Mr. Paxton whom you dislike."

What to Watch for. How do the players go about convincing Clint of the validity of their points of view? Do they realize that talking to him alone, without a third person, can accomplish a great deal more? Watch for manipulation from both Nancy and the teacher-player. Are they giving Clint breathing room to make his own decisions? Or are they pressuring him? Are they using unfair tactics? Watch for leveling in a sincere tone that speeds the action or nonleveling that slows it down. Are put-downs or sarcasm being used? How is the Clint-player reacting to this? How is the Clint-player handling his role? If some form of manipulation is used, how is the Clint-player reacting?

Discussion Following the Roleplay. Ask the Clint-player if he felt pressured by either of the other players. Did he feel free to make his own decision? Was he drawn to one player more than the other because of the way that one presented facts? If put-downs or sarcasm were used, was the Clint-player influenced against the person using them? Discuss how the Nancy-player and the teacher-player tried to convince Clint of their points of view. Was each willing to compromise? If leveling or nonleveling was evident, bring out the difference it made. Ask the audience's reaction to this. How did the Clint-player handle his role? Did he manage to listen to one player without antagonizing the other? If neither of the other players thought of asking to talk to him alone, did the Clint-player suggest to one or the other that he would like to do this? Was he able to do it in a gentle way without hurting or antagonizing?

Don't forget the games at the end of this chapter and also the games on understanding (pp. 58 and 63); they can aid in the search for a well-balanced personality.

FREE TO BE ONESELF

Roleplay 11

*Sally: At sixteen Sally has already received a high school degree. Her parents felt she was too young to attend college, so Sally had found a job to earn the money to continue her education. She has insisted on living with her sister in an apartment along with some other girls. She loves her parents but realizes they tend to prevent her from growing up.

Mr. Brown: Father of the girl. He resents his daughter's moving into an apartment instead of saving her money by living at home. He feels she does not appreciate the value of money. He is hurt that she would want to live away from home.

Mrs. Brown: Mother of the girl. She does not believe her daughter is mature enough to be on her own. She misses her baby!

[The scene opens in the family car, where the mother has been waiting. Father and daughter have just come from the police station where the father has paid his daughter's fine so that she will not have to spend the night in jail.]

Sally: Thanks, Dad. I'm sorry to bother you but there didn't seem to be anything else to do.

Father: That's what a father is for.

Sally: Thanks just the same. It's hard to believe, but we had no part in the rioting; we were just going to our apartment.

Mother: Police don't usually pick up anyone without a reason.

Sally: They said it was because we shouldn't have been on the street after the order to disperse.

Father: Are you trying to tell me the police would arrest you for just going home?

Sally: Yes, Dad. That's exactly what I mean.

---

*Role-descriptions and dialogue are for the conductor only; they are given as guides.

Suggestions for the Roleplay "Free to be Oneself"

Selecting Your Players. This is a conflict role. Equal fighting abilities are desirable but identification with the roles is even more desirable—if you can find players who can identify. The parent roles here are to bring out the Parent Ego State (see p. 99) of your players. A girl with nurturing tendencies and a boy with an authoritarian parent will make the role move more easily; but they are not necessary. The true nature of your player's Ego State is often not discernible until after the roleplaying has started. Occasionally this will cause a reversal of roles and blocking-out of instructions. All this is part of what makes roleplaying interesting.

Instructing Your Players. This role is to show how preconceived ideas (fair or unfair) can hamper understanding. The role is based on a true incident. In a student housing area of a midwestern town, a riot occurred when police tried to stop an illegal block party. Many of the students (and even some adults) who had taken no part in the riot were arrested. Remember, the role-descriptions and dialogue given are for the conductor. They are given not just to set forth the facts but to help the conductor get his players into the mood and conflict of the role.

You could say something like this to the daughter-player: "You graduated from high school at sixteen and were perfectly capable of going on to college but your parents felt you were too young. Now you are holding a job capably and living on your own and they still treat you like a baby. You need to get away from their protective custody to be able to grow." Help her to step easily into the role by setting the scene: "Dad had paid your bail but had said nothing in the station. You had tried to jolly him out of a black mood but he wasn't responding. You follow him out of the station and see your mother in the car with that 'my poor baby' expression. She is opening the car door for you."

From your mother-player you should be trying to call forth the nurturing or protective instinct. Be creative. Convince the mother-player that her daughter is too immature to be on her own. Use examples from your own experience. It could run something like: "Your daughter is trying to fly before her wings are fully grown. You allowed her to be on her own because she was so insistent, but had it been wise? Are you being a responsible parent? Being allowed to eat an atrocious diet and ruin her clothes is one thing, but being arrested for rioting is something else again. Are you shirking your parental duties?" Bring your player into the scene with: "There she is, coming out of the station and laughing as if it's all a joke. She's such a baby! You open the car door and she gets in."

From the father-player you are trying to bring forth a sense of being hurt because his daughter prefers to live away from home. Say something like this: "Your daughter has no concept of money. She'll spend a dollar to get five dollars' worth or to get a dime's worth—it's all the same to her. She ought to be

87

saving her salary for her education. But let Dad provide for that! Bring home the money, that's all kids expect from the old man these days!" Etc. And to plunge him into the role you might say: "You paid the bail and are now walking out to the car. You hadn't said anything in the police station in front of all those people, but now you're going to insist that your daughter come home. You open the car door on the driver's side."

What to Watch for. Watch how your parent-players pick up your instructions. Does the father-player play the role as an authoritarian parent? He will respond in the way he has learned from his parents. Does the mother-player play the nurturing parent or is she reasonable about her daughter's living on her own? Are they leveling about the facts and about their feelings? Is sensitive listening taking place? Do any of the players use active listening (i.e., giving sensitive feedback)? Is the daughter-player showing her need to be an independent person? Is she aware of the love and concern of the parent-players or only of her own need to be free?

Discussion after the Roleplay. Discuss what the young people feel the role of the parent should be. Is there a right and a wrong way of helping the developing teenager? How much freedom should a teenager be allowed? How many rights do the parents have? If a compromise was worked out in the roleplay, how does the audience feel about it? Discuss how the players used your instructions. Were they reasonable and honest about their feelings? Did the players' way of playing parents complicate the action? Bring up where leveling speeded up the action and where nonleveling slowed things down. Were any of the players left with a hurt or unsatisfied feeling? If any parallel speaking (see p. 17) took place, discuss it.

UNFAIR LOSS OR UNDESERVED HONOR

Roleplay 12

*Koren: A ninth grader, beginning her last year in junior high. Koren always checks the bulletin board before leaving for home. Officers for the Girls' Athletic Association will be posted, and she expects to be chosen president. She glances at the board and cannot believe her eyes. *Darlene* is listed as president of both the student council and the GAA! Koren's name does not even appear as a lesser officer. She is by far the best girl athlete, even if she isn't a top scholar. This isn't fair! She sees Darlene coming down the hall and hurries away. She has no desire to talk to her or anyone. Darlene is popular with the students and teachers, but that doesn't mean she's the best athlete!

Darlene: Also a junior high senior, Darlene has just found out that she's been chosen council president by the students. She is expecting her best friend, Koren, to be named president of the GAA, since Koren is by far the best athlete. They can celebrate together. As Darlene approaches the bulletin board, she sees Koren and calls out to her. Koren gives her an angry look before taking off at a run. Darlene looks at the board and finds her name listed as president of both groups; Koren is not even mentioned.

[Darlene hurries after Koren and manages to catch up. Although Koren will not even look at her, Darlene feels she must talk.]

Darlene: Gosh, Koren, don't be sore at me just because some of the teachers are stupid.

Koren: I'd rather not talk about it.

Darlene: Okay. I can understand how you feel. I just wanted you to know how I feel. I wasn't even expecting to be chosen as an officer of GAA, much less president.

Koren: But it's nice to be chosen isn't it?

Darlene: Yes, I'm human. But I feel better about being elected to the council by students than picked by teachers for the GAA. I'm a good athlete, but you're outstanding! I suppose it seems unfair to you.

Koren: You bet it does!

Darlene: I feel uncomfortable. Perhaps we could talk to one of the teachers.

Koren: Teacher's pet would think of that!

Darlene: They might give an explanation. I really can't understand it.

*Role-descriptions and dialogue are for the conductor only; they are given as guides.

Suggestions for the Roleplay "Unfair Loss or Undeserved Honor"

Selecting Your Players. Your players should be of equal fighting ability. The role will be more interesting if you can find a player (or players) who has (have) had an experience like the one here. If you don't know whether any in your audience have had such experiences, you might ask for volunteers.

Instructing Your Players. You are trying to instill confidence in each player about the role she is to play, and your tone of voice and "body language" will help you do this. You should also try to heighten the conflict. To Koren you might say: "You won't ever want Darlene as a friend again. You can't stand the sight of her. She has the position that is rightfully yours. Everyone knows this and you hate her! It isn't fair! It just isn't fair!" Etc. Remember to bring her into the scene with something like: "You see Darlene coming and you leave. You don't want to talk to her. She runs and catches up to you. That doesn't mean you have to talk to her. You suppose she feels very smart being chosen president of the council *and* the GAA."

To Darlene you could say: "Why is Koren sore at *you*? You didn't expect to be president. It made you feel uncomfortable. You two have been close friends since childhood. Can't she at least talk to you about it? Isn't she being unfair?" Etc. And to plunge her into the scene: "Once out of the building, you run to catch up with Koren. She won't talk and looks as if she is sulking. How childish can she be?"

Be creative about your instructions. Add what you can to increase the conflict or to help a player. Try to keep your help equal or to give more help to a lightweight player. Remember you are trying to bring out what it feels like to be treated unfairly or to win when you don't deserve to. Encourage your players to play their roles the way they are feeling them.

What to Watch for. Everyone will lose out many times during a lifetime—and many of these losses will be unfair. Both undeserved honors and losses bring on feelings that are difficult to handle and often hidden. This roleplay will give your players a chance to expose bad feelings, without putting anyone under actual pressure. Leveling is important here, but so is the ability to release feelings without antagonizing. The dialogue given shows how leveling helps get at the problem almost immediately. If you have sparked a real conflict or triggered some experience, your players may be kept from leveling by their resentments. Resentment may also prevent sensitive listening. In the role-dialogue given here the sarcastic remarks indicate resentment. Watch for this type of remark, as well as put-downs and overstatements, from the player with the unfair loss. Do they indicate resentment? Are they showing hurt feelings or some other hidden message? Is the resentment in the player with the unfair loss causing her to close off any genuine concern from her opponent? Is the undeserving winner using sensitive listening to be aware of the reason behind such remarks? Or is she thinking only of her own feelings?

Discussion Following the Roleplay. Discussion should be started by giving both players in the cast a chance to tell how they felt and why they reacted as they did (if they can). Did either of them recall an actual experience? If so, did the player or players level about the emotion they were feeling? If not, can they do so in the discussion? Was either player judgmental? Were "You-Messages" (see p. 18) used rather than "I-Messages"? What did the audience think of the way the players reacted? Discuss resentment. How it colors what we say, and why it makes it hard to level. Discuss the type of sensitive listening that hears hurt and resentment behind sarcastic remarks and overstatements. Does knowing the hidden reason for such remarks make it easier to avoid retaliating and help deal with them in a gentle way?

THE ROYAL ORDER OF THE SYMBOL
Game 5

AIM: To inspire ideals and goals.

MATERIALS: A sword, photocopies of the names for each player.

PEP TALK: (Give orally using own creativeness to add to it.)

"Life can be just as interesting and exciting as we want it to be. To be this way, however, it must have aim and direction, and it must be individualized for each one of us as persons. Everyone has certain 'givens' and 'talents,' but it's up to us as individuals to look within ourselves to find them and develop them. A good way to do this is to choose ideals and set goals to work for. In the game, you will be picking a name as a symbol to reflect the ideal or goal that you choose."

Game Action:

As a place to start ask your participants to examine their "givens," their interests, talents, and abilities. How can they use them to make a more exciting life? What profession, hobby, occupation, or avocation will use these "givens" to advantage? What skills, characteristics, or even virtues will be needed to carry this through? Have they need of some special trait to give them self-confidence or make their goal possible? What do they need to get the most out of life? Give each of your participants a list of names and ask them to pick a name that will reflect their interests in some way. This can be either as a profession or work, or a trait they believe advantageous to acquire.

Help Them to Think It Through in this Manner:*

1. Do you like people and like to be with them?
   You might enjoy being a *personnel director*, a *nurse*, or a *social worker*. If so, you would need to be *keen-eared*, *kind*, *merciful*, and a *comforter*. Or would you rather be a salesperson? Here you will need to be *cheerful*, *optimistic*, and perhaps *beguiling*.

2. Are you fascinated by a certain subject or profession?
   You might want to be an *actor* or *actress*, and would need *talent*, need to learn to *speak well* and be *vivacious*.

---

*Note: the italicized words can be found in the name-meaning lists (pp. 95-97).

Or maybe a *dancer* who would need to be *graceful, gifted,* and *lively.* Or perhaps be *exotic* or like a *flame.*

You might want to be an *ecologist* or *historian,* and would need to be *zealous* and *industrious.*

Or a *prophetess,* a *doctor,* or a *minister,* and would need to be *wise, helpful capable,* and *adept.*

3. Do you like action and adventure?

   You might like to be in the *coast guard,* a *Marine, Wac,* or *game hunter* and would need to be *brave* and *bold.*

4. Do you have *musical talent, craftmanship,* or *mechanical ability,* or an addiction to *writing?*

   To succeed here you will have to acquire *endurance,* become *resolute, unwavering,* and *patient.*

5. How about a political *leader* who would need to acquire *venerable wisdom, honesty,* and be *steady* and *righteous?*

6. Anyone for a *wife* who is *tender, lovable,* and *loving?* Or a mother who should be *gentle, serene,* and *motherly?*

7. Or a *husband* who is *helpful, courteous, faithful?* Or a *father* who is *kind* and *steady?*

   (Note suggestions in parentheses under occupation meanings [p. 96] and use them to stimulate players who have problems. If another sex will help for a specific meaning, change name to comply. Remember the name is only the symbol used, so if it becomes necessary create a new name.[2])

After names are chosen, pick a Grand Vizier, preferably someone who has chosen the category of a leader. He or she will find out the name, and the meaning of the name, of each of the players. Then the Grand Vizier will ask each player in turn to kneel and will touch each player's shoulders with a sword. She or he will dub each supplicant with the chosen name beginning with "Sir" for each boy and "Duchess" for each girl, giving a short spiel about the category of the chosen name.

Examples: 1. "I dub you 'Sir Wylie.' This gives me great pleasure for never have I met anyone so charming and beguiling."
2. "I dub you 'Duchess Thelma' for your wonderful nursing has saved many of my knights."

After everyone has had a turn, the Grand Vizier will say: "New knights and ladies of the Royal Order of the Symbol, you have been given a new name. It is up to you to see that the name performs its magic for you. You will spend a few seconds each day in affirming its purpose. Sit quietly and think of the name, declare its meaning positively, intellectualize it, feel it. Think of someone you admire who has this quality, or is in this position. Daydream of using it, of being caught up in it actively. Picture its accomplishment." The Grand Vizier will use his own name as an example:

1. "I would like to be a political leader so I chose the name Nestor which means 'venerable wisdom.' I will need to sense the underlying truth, and know what will be good for my country. Because of my strong desire for wisdom, I begin to feel wise on a deeper subconscious level. I think of Gandhi and Churchill. I try to picture myself like them. I see myself among a group of legislators trying to make a decision. I then picture myself hearing what has resulted from this decision, and I have a warm feeling of knowing I have done well." Or

2. "My name is Omar; I'm an architect. An architect plans a building, and works with people to construct it. I feel the joy of creating something beautiful. I see an architect I admire very much. I try to picture myself in his place. I can see myself working in close harmony with other people to bring these ideas to fruition. I can see majestic buildings I have designed." Or

3. "My name is Ada; I'm joyous. Joyous is being cheerful and loving life. I feel the sensation of joy permeate my being. I can see my friend Mary who is always bubbling with joy and I try to picture myself like her. I can see myself bringing joy to those around me. I daydream that the quality now has become a part of me, and my friends like to be near me so they can share my joy."

The Grand Vizier asks everyone to sit down and try it out for practice. Each will do it silently while the Vizier speaks:

"Sit comfortably! Quiet down! Think of your new name; its meaning. Elaborate on the meaning, finding other words to describe it." (Allow a few seconds to pass.) "Feel the emotion, the action, the being of it!" (Pause.) "Picture a person who has the quality you admire, or need, or is the best in the field you hope to be in. Picture yourself in that person's place. Daydream of a situation where you are using the quality, or are active in a project involving your name's meaning." (Pause.) "Now picture a time when you are at ease using the quality and picture also the pleasure it gives you. Or picture the work your hands or your brains have constructed.

"Remember that mind is the builder. As we seek, we find; as we knock, we are heard. What you can conceive, you can do. If your desire is strong enough, you can bring it into being. Positive thinking has a magic of its own."

Names to Inspire Boys

alert—Bryce
ardent—Ignatz
brave—Kimball
bright—Osbert
champion—Neil
cheerful—Tate
eager—Arden
famous—Elmer
fiery—Brant
free—Kermit
friend—Alvin
friendly—Elmo
foxy—Todd
gentle—Kevin
harmony—Alan
helper—Alexis
honest—Drew
kind—Holden
lively—Vivian
lucky—Felix
manly—Andrew
merry—Hilary
noble—Albert
order—Cosmo
rich—Otto
safe—Titus
sincere—Ernest
strong—Arthur
sunlike—Samson
wise—Conroy

a fighter—Boris
ambitious—Abelard
bold—Archibald
comforter—Nahum
courteous—Curtis
dextrous—Dexter
enduring—Durand
exceptional—Angus
faithful—Dillon
formidable—Egan
genuine—Sterling
growing—Vernon
honorable—Jarvis
industrious—Emmet
keen-eared—Otis
learner—Prentiss
lovable—Erastus
majestic—Augustus
merciful—Clement
outstanding—Jethro
patriotic—Leopold
peaceful—Culver
pleasant—Farand
powerful—Richard
renowned—Rodney
respected—Eldon
steadfast—Ethan
stronger—Xenos
vigilant—Gregory
valiant—Farrel

beguiling—Wylie
beloved—David
bright fame—Robert
capable, adept—Druce
charming—Wylie
clear one—Clarence
earthy—Adam
flame—Edan
heroic—Curran
illustrious—Clarence
kingly—Eric
laughter—Isaac
laurels—Lawrence
life—Hyman
lionlike—Llewelyn
longed for—Saul
mighty as a bear—Barrett
old in counsel—Eldred
pledge—Homer
renowned ruler—Roderick
shining light—Sinclair
shining of mind—Hubert
sophisticated—Desmond
steady—Hector
the greatest—Maximilian
unswerving—Hector
unwavering—Constantine
venerable wisdom—Nestor
watchful—Ira
young, virile—Colin

artist (painter)—Terrel
baker (caterer)—Baxter
brickmaker—Tyler
builder—Omar
  (contractor, architect)
chief—Cedric, Malvin
  (executive, magistrate,
  administrator, etc.)
chief, nobleman—Earl
  (federal cabinet officer)
cowman—Byron
craftsman—Wright
  (artisan, carpenter)
deep thinker—Edsel
gamekeeper—Warren
guide—Guy, Wyatt, Guyon
helper of men—Alexander
hunter—Falkner, Monte
  (detective, G man)
increaser (father)—Joseph
latheworker—Turner
  (machinist, die maker)
leader—Duke
liberator—Lysander
minstrel—Baird
one who summons—Sumner
oracle (prophet)—Phineas
peacemaker—Wilfred
poet (journalist)—Devin
roofmender—Thatcher
sailor—Murray, Murdock
scholar—Culbert
teacher—Enoch, Latimer
  (guru, trainer, coach)
warrior—Luther, Roger
worker in stone—Mason
  (sculptor, geologist)
world power—Donald

adviser—Redmond
  (business specialist, personnel
  director, lawyer, social worker)
arrow maker—Fletcher
candle maker—Chandler
chief, guardian—Howard
  (inspector, sheriff, fire chief)
chief of the valley—Kendall
  (mayor, governor, etc.)
coast defender (coastguardsman)—Seward
dove keeper—Coleman
farmer—Fabian, Barth, George
  (agronomist, agriculture professor)
guardian, warder—Parry
  (prison, port, or fire warden;
  caretaker; museum custodian)
healer—Asa, Galen, Jason
  (doctor, psychiatrist, medical
  technician, minister)
lover of the earth—Demetrius
  (environmentalist, ecologist)
people's ruler (president)—Theodoric
protector—Edmund, Richmond
  (policeman, fireman, ranger)
record keeper—Chauncey
  (accountant, registrar, scribe,
  bookkeeper, clerk, chronicler,
  genealogist, computer operator)
sea leader (commodore)—Marmaduke
speaker, interpreter—Driscoll
  (actor, preacher, commentator)
storekeeper (owner, clerk)—Spencer
  (grocery, drug, hardware, furniture,
  or department store)
wagonmaker (cars, trucks)—Wayne
war guardian (guardsman)—Hilliard
weaver (rugs, cloth)—Webster
  (manufacturer, designer, worker)

Names to Inspire Girls
Occupation, Avocation

beautiful—Linda
dainty—Mignon
fertile—Pomona
fiery—Brenda
flame—Bren
free—Fanny
gentle—Mildred
gifted—Pandora
graceful—Grace
helper—Alexis
helpmate—Sacha
honest—Amena
just—Justina
kind—Pamela
life—Eve, Vita
lively—Vivian
lovable—Amanda
loving—Mabel
lucky—Gada
motherly—Rhea
pleasant—Naomi
pleasing—Hedy
rainbow—Iris
rebel—Asiyah
reborn—Renee
rejoice—Kay
a song—Carmen
speech—Amira
spring—Aviva
a star—Esther
striving—Amelia
strong—Irma
tender—Morna
truthful—Alice
untamed-Wilda
wisdom—Ophelia
wise—Belinda
zealous—Ardis

ambitious—Beverly
beloved—Darlene
born free—Camilla
brave—Bernadine
brilliant—Alberta
cautious—Prudence
charming—Dulcie
cheerful—Allegra
desirable—Willa
faithful—Fidelia
fervent—Ernestine
good luck—Holly
gracious—Roanna
happy—Ida, Felice
hardworker—Ilka
harmony—Concordia
honorable—Noreen
hospitable—Zenia
industrious—Emily
joyous—Ada, Narda
logical—Akilah
majestic—Augusta
married—Beulah
merciful—Mercedes
optimistic—Nadine
pledge—Gize
promise—Giselle
rejuvenation—Edna
resolute—Constance
righteous—Camilla
serene—Delphine
speak well—Eulalie
spry sprite—Disa
steady—Pierrette
talented—Pandora
vivacious—Tallulah
well-known—Lara
womanly—Charlotte

adviser (lawyer?)—Monica
authority (boss?)—Hazel
battlemaid (Wac?)—Matilda
be successful—Barika
chief (manager?)—Melvina
commander—Hazel
composer—Edda
earth lover—Georgiana
friend of mankind—Sandra
gardenworker—Hortense
girl of forest—Silvia
glorious leader—Kim
God-consecrated—Isabel
harvester—Teresa
helper of men—Alexandra
historian—Clio
home mistress—Harriet
horse lover—Philippa
magic dancer—Satinka
messenger—Angela
mother—Ambika
musical—Cecilia
nursing—Thelma
one who heals—Emma
pattern (model)—Norma
peacemaker—Wilfreda
prophetess—Cassandra
protectress (cop)—Ramona
ruler (politico)—Roderica
scientific—Haley
sea maiden (Wave)—Alima
sea protector—Meredith
strong worker—Millicent
the greatest—Maxine
tower of strength—Magda
trader—Yarkona
watchwoman—Greer
weaver—Penelope

P A C PINBALL

Game 6

PLAYERS: The game is best played with from four to six players.

MATERIALS: Heavy cardboard (coat box); colored paper and paste; stapler or staple gun; bright flashlight; scotch tape, paper, and pencil. Noisemaker optional.

AIM OF THE GAME: To get your participants in touch with their Ego States. The game will be played by answering questions as honestly as possible. Explain to the players that the Ego States brought up in the game are not necessarily good or bad; all are necessary for a balanced life. The players will keep their own records, so encourage them to be honest. If they feel a guilty or negative feeling in regard to some of the questions, have them note where and bring it up in discussion.

Building the "Machine" (this can be done beforehand):

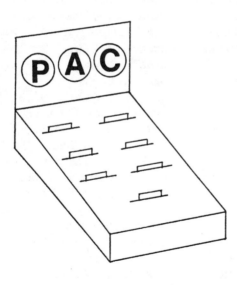

Take the bottom half of a cardboard coat box and cut off a small amount of each long side to give it a slight bevel. Cut part off one of the ends to match the level of the long sides. Invert the box keeping the short end in front, and cut in slits for the insertion of cards. For the headboard, cut a section out of the box's top; the headboard should stand up at least twice as high as the base. In the top of the headboard, cut three circles the size of a flashlight lens. Cover each hole with colored paper using a different color for each. Cut the letters *P*, *A*, and *C* out of black paper; paste one on each of the colored circles. Staple the completed headboard to the base.

(The machine is not absolutely necessary for the game. The conductor could just draw the circles on the blackboard and use colored chalk to outline a P, A, or C for emphasis. Or he could just express it verbally.)

Terminology of the Ego States (P, A, and C)

PARENT EGO STATE:[3] Taking on the attitudes and behavior of the people who have served as parent figures for the child.

> *nurturing parent*—protective, sympathetic, and supportive.
> *prejudicial parent*—critical, opinionated, chastising, and moralistic.

ADULT EGO STATE: "Feelings, attitudes and behavior patterns that are adapted to the current reality and are not affected by parental prejudices or archaic attitudes left over from childhood."[4]

CHILD EGO STATE:[5] Responding (to the inner world of feelings, experiences, and adaptations) in the same way you did as a child.

> *natural child*—Becoming the unrestrained infant still inside each person. (free-swinging, pleasure-loving, curious, sensual, impetuous, affectionate, but also rebellious, self-centered, and easily angered)
>
> *little professor*—Using the unschooled wisdom of the child, able to receive non-verbal messages and play hunches. (intuitive, creative, and manipulative)
>
> *adapted child*—Acting like a child who has modified natural inclinations to the demands of authority figures. (obedient, passive, anxious)

Play Action of the Game

Part 1. In this part of the game the players will be defining the area they wish to work in. Have them jot down the activities they engage in during a full year. Each player will choose ten items he or she is most interested in and spends the most time on. If a player spends a great deal of time on sports, her list might contain two or three different ones. If a player is a faithful watcher of TV, his list might have a number of programs. Another player's list might not have sports or TV at all.

> *Sports:* Football, Tennis, Swimming, Skiiing, Track, etc.
> *Lessons:* Musical Instruments, Singing, Dancing, etc.
> *Group Activities, Clubs:* Church Youth Groups, Debating, Choir, Cheerleading, Dramatics, Chemistry Club, etc.
> *Hobbies:* Photography, Coin or Stamp Collecting, etc.
> *Television* or *Reading:* News, Novels, Movies, TV Games, etc.

Part 2. As soon as one player is ready, start with him and allow the rest more thinking time. Of the ten items, have your player pick one that he spends a good deal of time with. Then start your game.

Have the player compute the amount of time he spends with this particular activity on a one to six point basis. Then have participant select one of the following answers:

I engage in this activity because:

1. I believe it's a sensible, logical thing to do. (A)
2. I think it is something I ought to do. (P)
3. I enjoy it—it's just for the pure joy of doing it (or watching it). (C)
4. My parents seem to like this sort of thing, and—it just seems the thing to do. (P)
5. My friends have joined and I enjoy being with them and doing what they are doing. (C)
6. It can teach me things that will probably help me later in life. (A)

(Explain to your participants that you realize their reason may not be listed here but ask them to choose the one that seems to apply the most or that seems to carry the most weight with them.)

After your player has chosen one of the reasons listed, note the letter in parenthesis by it, and light this up on the machine by holding the flashlight behind it. Flash the light on and off and rattle the noisemaker if you have one.

Have your player jot down the letter the machine flashes and, under it, the time-rating (1 to 6) he gave the activity. Then have him look at the other activities on his list. Does he engage in any of them for the same reason as the first? If so, have him compute a time-rating for each and list the number(s) under the same letter. For the remaining activities on his list, have him repeat the whole process. At the end he will have three columns—P, A, and C—each with numbers under it.

Here is an example to make this clear:

Joan has chosen to start with *Cheerleading*. She practices her motions and cheers whenever she gets a chance. Her father has put a mattress in the den so she can practice tumbling. 6 points doesn't seem right, but cheerleading is her main interest right now, and she feels right about rating it 5 points. As to her reason for cheerleading, there's no question—the pure joy of doing it! The machine records "C."

Joan looks over her other activities and decides she started *Dancing* for the same reason. She gives herself 3 points for this—she doesn't spend as much time with it. Now her score is: C

5

3.

Joan looks at her *Tennis* item. She enjoys playing it, and is on the courts from the beginning of the season until the end. A 6 for time spent doesn't seem unreasonable. However, Joan doesn't feel the same about tennis as she does about cheerleading and dancing. Right from the beginning she had a special aptitude for tennis and a drive to excel in it. Having won every contest she has entered, Joan is even toying with the idea of becoming a professional. Joan asks to hear the options again. The first one, about its being logical doesn't sound too bad. But number 6—the idea that tennis was teaching her something that would help her later in life—seems better. Joan decides on that one and the machine responds with an "A." *Declamatory* was somewhat the same. She gives herself 2 for time spent on it.

Debating is her next item; she gives it a 4 for time spent. She isn't sure why she got involved in debating. Her father had been very good in it and had talked about it a lot. He felt it had helped him in his profession as a lawyer. So she supposed it must be option two or four—either something she ought to do, or something her parents liked. She decides on number four. The machine flashes "P" for this. *Band* seems similar, so she puts it under P and gives it 4 for time spent. For *Choir*, her next item, she considers her reasons and picks option two. The machine flashes "P"; so she puts it under P, giving it a 3 for time.

Most of the people Joan goes with are crazy about *Skiing*. She doesn't like it as well as other activities, but it is fun to be with the gang. So she picks option five for it and the machine flashes a "C"; she writes down 3 under C for time spent. She likes being with the gang watching *Football* too, but she enjoys watching the game itself more, so picks option three for it. The machine again flashes "C." She gives it a 2 for time spent, and writes this under C. Joan loves *Movies* and fictional shorts on television and watches whenever there is time—which isn't too often. So she gives this a 2 for time spent, and puts the 2 under the C, since she considers movies like football.

Joan's score now looks something like this:

P	A	C
4	6	5
4	2	3
3		3
		2
		2
11	8	15.

Part 3. Have the participants answer the following questions[6] on the basis of how often they occur—giving from one to six points for each answer. A negative answer will, of course, be no points. Continue to itemize the points under the letter the machine will flash. (If they do not participate in group activities, have them answer in the context of what they do every day.)

101

1. In the activities you especially like, is everything cut and dried where new ideas are not encouraged? (P)
2. When faced with a problem in your activities do you tend to avoid it or try to pretend it isn't there? (C)
3. Do your classmates accuse you of being too serious and not entering into the fun of the activity? (A)
4. If you are not a leader of a group, do you accept the ideas of the leader without expressing differences when you feel them? (C)
5. Do you keep yourself so busy with projects in the clubs and elsewhere that you have no time for fun, or for just doing nothing? (A)
6. Instead of entering wholeheartedly into projects or activities, do you claim you don't know how when you just don't want to make the effort? (C)
7. If you are one of the leaders of the club, do you find yourself telling your classmates that they "ought to" or "should" do a project the way you want it done? (P)
8. Can you sometimes picture yourself as a machine that is just spitting out data, computerized analysis, or decisions? (A)
9. Do you find yourself expressing your parents' value judgments rather than applying your own thoughts and examination to the subject matter? (P)

After your player has time-rated all of the questions, have him ask the machine for the letter involved. Note the letter in parenthesis after each question and light up this letter on the machine. As your player receives the letter for each question, have him add the time-rated number for each to the columns he has made for Part 2.

Part 4. Bring everyone together for the final stage. Remind your players that this is only a game. It is not meant to be exact; circumstances could alter the answers and lack of honesty could distort them. The aim is only to acquaint the players with the different Ego States, and give a "ball park" estimate of your players' Ego States.

Have the participants count up their scores. Then have them draw circles for the letters P, A, and C, each in proportion to the total score for that letter.[7]

Look once again at Joan:
Joan realizes that her "A" is a good size and her "P" certainly isn't small; but her "C" seems to be in balance—or should it be larger for this time in life?

Joan glances over at her friend, Bob. She likes him a lot because he is so much fun. He has a huge circle for "C," not too large a one for "P," but his "A" is nonexistent! Bob has laughingly said he will probably just be a bum when he gets out of school. It sounded like fun when he kidded about it! She notices now that he is looking at his drawing with some concern.

Her friend Susan has a different picture. Joan had thought of Susan when the question came up about how classmates accuse you of being too serious and not entering into the fun. That certainly fit Susan! Her "A" is very large, and her "P" is even larger. Her "C" is the one that is very small. Susan is looking at her picture with surprise.

Joan notices that Dale's picture doesn't seem to be like him. If he did his figuring in as sloppy a manner as he did that project last week, it's no wonder. But after all it's only a game! Gus and Martha and most of the rest have large "C's" and reasonable-sized "P's." Some of their "A's" are small though. But this is supposed to be a fun time in life, isn't it?

There should be some discussion with this game. The questions in Part 4 are on the Constant Ego State (a small distortion of the normal). If these questions do not apply, players should be able to pass them by with negative answers. If anyone has a guilty or negative feeling about a certain question, ask that person if he can figure out why. Is it like a parent looking over their shoulder telling them they are wasting their time? Is it like a child resenting an implied censor?

Explain to your teenagers they are at a crossroad in life and can start to bring their Ego States into balance. Their child should be allowed to come out and play freely with abandon. They should also be growing more aware of the adult within them who can stop and reassess the past, and, looking at the present objectively, use reasoning powers to plan on a reality basis.

Listing as a Discussion Technique: What Is Maturity?

(Taken from Ann Landers)[8]

1. Maturity is the ability to control anger and settle differences without violence or destruction.

2. Maturity is patience. It is the willingness to pass up immediate pleasure in favor of the long-term gain.

3. Maturity is perseverance, the ability to sweat out a project or a situation in spite of heavy opposition and discouraging setbacks.

4. Maturity is the capacity to face unpleasantness and frustration, discomfort and defeat, without complaint or collapse.

5. Maturity is the ability to make a decision and act. However, action without careful thought can be as bad as inaction. The mature person takes the time to consider realistic possibilities, and consequences.

6. When a decision turns out to be wrong, maturity is being big enough and humble enough to say, "I was wrong," and change. And, when right, the mature person need not experience the satisfaction of saying, "I told you so."

7. Maturity means dependability, keeping one's word, coming through the crisis. The immature are masters of alibi. They are the confused and disorganized. Their lives are a maze of broken promises, former friends, unfinished business, and good intentions that somehow never seem to materialize.

8. Maturity is the art of living in peace in spite of that which we cannot change.

(Maturity is a controversial subject where no two people agree. The reader will have his own ideas; so will the teenagers! Teenagers are constantly coming up against the word "immature." Some discussion on the subject should be beneficial.)

Suggested reading:
Muriel James and Dorothy Jongeward, *Born to Win* (Reading, Mass.: Addison-Wesley Publishing Co., 1971).

6

the love-marriage-divorce syndrome

The need to love and be loved starts the moment a child is born and continues throughout his or her life. There are many types of love and all of them play a part in the life of a teenager. The most troublesome, however, is the mating instinct.

Carl Jung sees "first love" or "love at first sight" as a transference. There is, Jung says, a feminine ideal or image in each man, which he calls an *anima*, and a masculine image in every woman, which he calls an *animus*. Ordinarily, in adolescence we project this image onto a qualified person, and have the earth-shaking experience of "falling in love." When the projection is withdrawn the love is ended. This is commonly called "puppy love" and most young people experience it numerous times. Projection alone may be the reason "behind a lifetime of many loves."[1] Real love, although it may start with projection, becomes deepened and cannot be as easily withdrawn.

Whether it stems from projection or not, however, an unrequited love can cause shattering pain and bitterness. Roleplaying can bring emotional release; and the discussion following can alert the players to the fact that almost everyone goes through the pangs of unrequited love but grows in understanding from it.

EARLY MARRIAGE

Roleplay 13

*Jean: Jean realizes that her teenage marriage has not been working out the way she thought it would. Her husband has been spending more and more time with the boys. She is unhappy and disillusioned. This is why she agreed when he said he wanted a divorce. But what happened? Is there something wrong with her? She *had* tried.

Lester: Lester realizes that he should never have married so young. He had been so much in love that he had needed to have Jean belong to him. Now all that feeling is gone and he just doesn't like being married. He would rather be with the boys. She is a nice girl and he hates to hurt her feelings. He feels guilty about that. However, he is simply not in love with her any more. Come what may, he wants out!

[As the scene opens Jean and Lester are discussing a trip she was to make home. She had thought a separation might be an answer. She now realizes it would make no difference.]

Jean: Be honest with me, Lester. You'd be glad to see me go and just stay away, wouldn't you?

Lester: I guess our marriage isn't working out so well.

Jean: Is it the responsibility? I have a job now and I'll keep working. We don't need to have any children unless you want them.

Lester: It's not that, Jean. You've been wonderful. It's not your fault.

Jean: But then why? Why?

Lester: I don't know, Jean. I don't like being married. I like being with the boys, and I don't like feeling guilty. I just don't know why the marriage hasn't worked out for me.

*Role descriptions and dialogue are for the conductor only; they are given as guides.

106

Suggestions for the Roleplay "Early Marriage"

Selecting Your Players. Nothing special here. The girl and the boy should be of equal fighting ability. If one or the other must be a lightweight player, it should be the role of the boy.

Instructing Your Players. Remember not to tell your players what to say. You should be trying to give them the facts of the role and some psychological help to put them into the mood of it. To Jean you could say something like: "You wonder what happened to your marriage. Did you do something wrong? Lester had been *so* in love with you. You've tried hard to make it a success. How have you failed? Is there something about *you* that killed his love?" Etc. And to bring her into the scene: "You had thought a short separation might help the marriage—maybe even bring back that wonderful feeling of closeness. Now you are convinced it wouldn't make any difference. But you feel you've got to talk it out. You have to know what happened and there's no better time than right now. You're so terribly lonely!" Etc.

To Lester you could say: "You want out of this marriage—but quick! There's nothing wrong with Jean; she's a great gal. But all the ecstasy of being with her is gone—there just isn't anything left! You would rather be with the boys!" Etc. And to plunge him into the scene: "You're glad Jean is leaving on this trip. After she's gone for a while it might be easier to urge her to seek a divorce. You really don't want to hurt her, but you can't stand living without freedom! And you're lonely besides." Etc.

What to Watch for. This role deals with the boy's projection of his anima, his "puppy love." The players should be leveling with each other and trying to understand what has happened. Watch for the "there must be something wrong with me" feeling in the player of the girl-part. This has been built into the role. How is she handling it? Is she retaliating with put-downs? The role-dialogue given shows Jean on the defensive but not reacting in this way. It also shows leveling and how it brings the players quickly and directly to the problem they are facing. They should be trying to arrive at some solution that does not leave the girl-player with a feeling of rejection or the boy with a feeling of guilt. Does either player try to deal with the idea (given in the instructions) that they are feeling lonely? Do they try to answer why she is unhappy or he feels there is nothing left to the marriage? This part of the role is trying to get at maturity and the lack of intimacy between the couple.

Discussion Following the Roleplay. After the role is finished both players should be asked how they are feeling. If they feel rejected or guilty the roleplaying was not a complete success. Have each player state what he or she would like to have heard from the other player. Living together without marriage should be discussed and whether or not it would make any difference in how they would feel when they split up. If the conductor feels it will help, he can have one cast play the role as if married and another cast as if merely living together. The need for maturity when living together or planning marriage should be brought up and discussed. Discuss marriage itself. Its pros and cons. Discuss commitments and why business partners find it advantageous to have a written agreement.

Listing as a discussion technique can be used to advantage here. At the end of this chapter (p. 125) is the discussion question: "What is love?" "What is maturity?" (p. 104) is also especially appropriate for this roleplay. Also at the end of this chapter are games to emphasize the points brought up (pp. 120-124).

(The roleplays in this book are written to stimulate dialogue and communication, and almost anyone can use them. Many of the roles, however, can be changed by someone with counseling experience to meet the needs of more serious problems. This role, for example, could be strengthened to deal with serious rejection by changing the instructions to Jean: delete any mention of divorce. When Lester asks for a divorce in the roleplay it should come as a surprise to her. A person with counseling experience could also add other problems he would like to deal with.)

BROKEN PLANS FOR MARRIAGE

Roleplay 14

*Clay: Clay has been engaged since his junior year in high school. Janet, whom he loves deeply, has not only broken the engagement several times but keeps on postponing the wedding. Two months ago they set a date which was to have been next week. He had sent out invitations to all his friends. Now she has phoned him long distance telling him she will not marry him. He has tried to do everything he could for her, even giving up golfing which she did not like. He must have her. Life just won't be worth anything without her!

Janet: Janet, who is a graduating senior, isn't sure why she doesn't want to marry Clay. He would be a good provider and he will do almost anything she asks him to. There have been times when she felt she was in love with him. But this has only been when she was with him; afterwards she realizes something is wrong. Is it because she just does not love him enough? Or is it something else? How will she make Clay accept the fact that she will not marry him? Last time he sent out invitations to his friends to force her to set a date. This time she is sure and determined!

[Scene opens when Janet comes to answer the door late at night and finds Clay there. Clay has flown home not long after getting Janet's call. He has walked out on his performance at the ballet.]

Janet: Clay, you promised to finish what you had to do in New York before coming home. Did you leave before the performance?

Clay: Aren't you going to ask me in?

Janet: Come in. [She walks into the room and sits down. He follows her and also sits down.] How do you think the new Director is going to take your leaving?

Clay: I really don't care. I can't perform unless everything is settled between us. I'm no good without you, Janet. I just can't live without you!

Suggestions for the Roleplay "Broken Plans for Marriage"

Selecting Your Players. Either the players should be equal in ability or greater weight should be given to the boy-player. An aggressive salesman-type boy would work well if you wish to highlight a person who gives in under pressure.

*Role-descriptions and dialogue are for the conductor only; they are given as guides.

109

Instructing Your Players. Try to help each of your players believe in the role he'll be playing and identify with it. To Clay you could say something like: "You are very deeply in love with Janet. Why does she keep torturing you by putting off the wedding? Come hell or high water you're going to make sure she marries you this time. These postponements are murder! They're upsetting your job and everything else." Etc. And to bring Clay into the scene: "At the door of Janet's house you hesitate. How are you going to convince Janet to stop this nonsense? You have the license—maybe you can convince her to elope with you tonight. How can she be moved in that direction? By the light jolly fun of an adventure? By proving your deep love in some way? Would she be influenced if you told her you'd commit suicide if she didn't marry you tonight?" Be creative! You are trying to get your player to manipulate.

To Janet you could say: "You don't know why you don't want to marry Clay, he seems everything a husband ought to be. But something is wrong, you have a gut-level feeling that shouts, 'No!' You don't want to hurt his feelings, but if you marry him you'll regret it for the rest of your life." Etc. And to bring her into the scene: "That night you open the door and there stands Clay. He must have missed his performance."

What to Watch for. The emphasis in this role is twofold: on the person who gives in although it is against a subconscious feeling to do so, and on the one who fights for what he wants even if he hurts everyone including himself. Watch for the player who will give in rather than bruise another's feelings. Notice where leveling is used and where it is not. The Janet-player should try to understand her own feelings against the marriage and level with Clay about them. (Reasons should come from player's experience.) Watch for what the players forget or ignore in the instructions. If the boy-player is the hard-sell-salesman type, watch for defensive actions on the part of the girl, or her inability to fight this type of manipulation. The boy-player is not playing a prop role. The role may trigger a feeling of rejection in him, changing the emphasis of the role.

Discussion Following the Roleplay. Discuss gut-level feelings. What are they? Is it wise to ignore them? How can you bring these feelings to the surface so that you can understand them? If two casts are used, which player handles the Janet-part better? Discuss the type of manipulation written into the boy-player's role. Why is it unfair? Why does it endanger happiness? How can the boy win, yet be the big loser? Discuss the aims of good marriages and why elements written into this role go against them. A prudent boy-player may choose to ignore some of the instructions and play the role as his conscience dictates. This is legitimate and should be discussed. Be careful not to condemn a player who in spite of how he felt used the instructions given.

THE NEED TO BE LOVED AND NEEDED

Roleplay 15

*Mother: Comes home from a bridge party and finds a note from her husband, Steve, saying he has a dinner appointment. She had a few cocktails at the card party so she just continues to drink. She wonders how her son Brien is. Are they teaching him self-sufficiency at the military academy? Does her boy need her now? Was her husband right when he said her love for the boy was ruining him?

Father: Coming home from a successful business appointment, he notices the lights are still on but hopes his wife, Ida, has gone to bed. He is too tired to deal with her foibles tonight. She certainly ought to have been able to find something to amuse herself—God knows he gives her enough money! Always fussing about the boy. Well, he misses their son as much as she does. And if she loves the boy as much as she says, she ought to be glad to do what's best for him. Her drinking is beginning to be a real problem.

Brien: He has run away from the academy because he has to know *why* he is being sent away to school. Is he so obnoxious that his parents can't even stand the sight of him? He'd shape up if his mother would only tell him what was wrong. If they loved him wouldn't their actions show it? As he enters the house, he notices his mother has been drinking so he slips up to his room. It would be better to talk to her in the morning.

[As Steve, the father, comes in the door, his wife comes to greet him with a drink in her hand. Brien comes down the stairs when he hears their voices.]

Mother: I'm glad you finally got home. I stayed up to have a talk with you.

Father: We'll talk in the morning. You sound as if you've had a little too much to drink.

Mother: I've had a lot to drink but I'm not drunk. I know because I still hurt.

Brien: (coming down the stairs) You're not the only one who's hurt, Mother. Neither one of you answered my letter about coming home.

Father: Are you in trouble?

Brien: No. I just have to know why I was sent away.

---

*Role-descriptions and dialogue are for the conductor only; they are given as guides.

Suggestions for the Roleplay "The Need to Be Loved and Needed"

Selecting Your Players. Your players should be of equal fighting ability. The part of Brien can of course be played by a girl. Say that she is being sent away to school even though a good high school is available near home. She could be called Rhoda.

Instructing Your Players. Try to give each of your players confidence in his role. But also try to heighten the conflict. After giving Brien, the boy-player, some of the facts, you might add something like: "You don't know why you pulled some of those dumb things, but it wasn't so that they would send you away. Can you make them understand that you don't know why you do these things? Can you tell them you need their love and understanding?" Etc. And to bring him into the scene: "After reaching your room, you hear both your father and your mother talking. You decide you might as well get this over tonight."

To the mother-player you could say something like: "Isn't it a mother's role to love a child? Besides, you have to compensate for a father who isn't sufficiently interested to spend time with the boy. A boy needs his father around—expecially for discipline." Etc. And to plunge her into the scene: "You hear the car, and then the door slam, and you go to the front hallway where your husband is taking off his coat. You've had just enough to drink to talk up to him!"

To the father-player you could say: "You earn the money—the very least she could do is amuse herself! Does she have any idea of the pressures you're under? You wish you had a tenth of the time off she wasted. You would have spent it with the boy. *You* could have given him love without smothering him! But she can't even discipline herself, much less the boy." Etc. And to bring him into the scene: "As you take off your coat and hat, your wife comes to greet you with a drink in her hand. How long has she been drinking? You are too tired to fight with her, so how can you talk her into going to bed?"

What to Watch for. The emphasis of this role is mainly on the boy-player's problem, so he should be sent in almost as soon as the parent-players start talking. The boy's need for love is built into the role. Young people often express their need for love by means of unacceptable behavior—if nothing else, it's sure to get attention! It's a manipulative technique, however, and young people are often unaware that they're doing it, so it is built into this role to bring it to attention. Is the boy-player aware that the parent-players also have problems? Is he trying to help in a constructive way?

The emphasis of the role is on love. Are the parent-players showing the boy-player love? Words alone may not be enough. The act of sending the child away to school says a lot more to him than their words may. How do the players overcome this? Watch for the way things are said. Do "body language" and tone of voice express any deep feeling? Do they convey concern? Is the boy-player, who is supposed to be receiving the love, actually feeling it? (This can be brought out in the discussion afterward, or the conductor can stop the playing and ask the boy-player how he is feeling.) The parent-players should try to show love and consideration toward each other as well as the boy.

The roles of the parents are more than prop roles. The youths playing them will tend to imitate their own parents, and will probably act this way later in real life. Watch for the player who takes the role of father as a "heavy" and makes little attempt to justify it. The mother-player may also see her role as an alcoholic without rights. This should be brought up in the discussion; ask members of the audience to tell how they would handle it. Two casts could also be comapred.

Discussion Following the Roleplay. The discussion with this role could center on love. Was each of the players *feeling* love? Were they given the feeling of being needed? (If love is not being felt, the conductor may want to play some of the practice games for showing love and concern given at the end of the chapter.) Did each of the players give as much as he could to the role? Was any player "snowed under" by the strong offense or defense of another player? Point out where leveling helped or where a lack of it slowed the action down. There might be a discussion on how non-verbal messages sometimes carry more weight than what is being said with words.

DID IT HAVE TO BE DIVORCE?

Roleplay 16

*Ben Boyd: Teenage boy whose parents have problems that might lead to divorce. His mother is a sensitive and understanding person but doesn't apply this to her husband. His father, although he means well, is not sensitive. At a summer job with his father's company, Ben had learned that his father is an excellent executive, but holds an exacting position in which there is constant pressure. This morning his father had asked him if he had taken any liquor out of the cabinet. He told him he hadn't, but afterwards wondered if he should have taken the blame. Mom was going to spring her new job on Dad tonight. That would be rough. Can he help in any way? Is he somehow to blame for their problems?

Ivy Boyd: Because of her husband's lack of consideration in front of people, it has been increasingly hard for Ivy to entertain or go to company parties. If it weren't for her university courses (which he considers harmless) she would have given up long ago. She now has a Ph.D. in bacteriology and has been offered a good job with a firm that knows and respects her work. She needs this, for her husband has made her feel unwanted and inadequate. But taking this position might cause a divorce. She debated whether she had the right to deprive five children of their father even if he didn't understand them. Finally, she accepted the position and now intends to fill it, come what may. In frustration she had accidentally smashed a number of bottles of liquor.

Guy Boyd: Guy is an executive in a large company. He wonders how he could have been so unlucky as to pick a wife with so little capacity to grow. Ivy's always talking about a job—what a laugh! She's so inadequate! Divorce might have been an answer, but he feels the children need him. She would certainly make a mess of their lives! He has noticed that she's been drinking more lately, but he was amazed when he checked the liquor cabinet. Is she an alcoholic?

[The scene opens after dinner when the children have taken off to various parts of the large home and the servants are waiting to clear the table. As they leave the dining room and enter the living room, Ivy turns to Guy.]

---

*Role-descriptions and dialogue are for the conductor only; they are given as guides.

Ivy: I'd like to talk to you about something, Guy. [He shrugs his shoulders and they sit down.] Once, when I wanted to work you embarrassed me in front of an employer. I have accepted a position with Kendal laboratories and I advise you not to interfere.

Guy: I give you plenty of money. You don't *need* to work. The place for a woman with children is in the home!

Suggestions for the Roleplay "Did It Have to Be Divorce?"

Selecting Your Players. This role has been structured so that teenagers can play all of the parts. Players can be of equal fighting ability, or, if your players are unmatched, the mother-player should be the lightweight and the father-player the heavyweight.

Instructing Your Players. Address your players in your own words; try to instill confidence in them for their roles and try to produce conflict. To the boy player you could say something like: "You love both your parents, and want to be with both of them. Is there anything you can do to prevent the divorce your mother has been talking about? Would it have helped if you had taken the blame for the liquor? You feel you should have been helping your parents in some way." Etc. And to bring him into the scene: "You have come back to the dining room to get your history book and you hear your parents talking in the living room. You stay to listen hoping you can help somehow." Conductor can tell the boy-player when to join the others or leave it up to him.

To the mother-player you could say: "You've put up with Guy tearing down your self-esteem long enough. Hired people take care of the work around the house and you need to feel valuable somewhere. The children are all in school and you can arrange your work so that you will be at home when they are. If Guy interferes in your taking the job in any way, you'll ask for a divorce. Children or no children—you've had it!" And to plunge her into the scene: "As you walk out of the dining room into the living room, you realize that Guy may be taking off shortly, so you might as well get it over with. Waiting won't make it any easier to tell him about the job." You are building in reluctance which a shy player might pick up.

To Guy, the father-player, you could say: "You've been forced to entertain your clients at a motel because your wife has refused to be a hostess. It's humiliating! You've put up with Ivy in a lot of things because of the children, but putting up with her as an alcoholic would be too much. You'd get custody of the children—they certainly didn't need a mother like that! Besides, you support a large family with a very demanding job, and you need a little understanding! You're lonely!" Etc. And to bring him into the scene: "You follow Ivy into the living room. You have a meeting later but first you've got to find out about that liquor." The father-role as cast is that of a dominant, opinionated person, but it will depend on the player as to how it is played.

What to Watch for. How does the boy try to help his parents? Does he try to take their problem on himself (or "own" their problem)? This is written into the role. Watch to see if this happens. Watch for both good and bad ways the boy tries to help. Perhaps he will try to help by taking the blame for the liquor. This may cause complications. Two people can usually work out a conflict more easily without a third person. Is the boy sensitive enough to understand this? Does he slow the action or help it? If the roleplay stagnates because of him, the conductor can send in another player to tell him he is needed elsewhere or call him to the phone.

Are all the players listening sensitively enough to be aware of the feelings behind the words of the others? Is there a hidden message they aren't hearing? Watch for leveling about the facts each player has received. Are they learning from each other by careful questioning and listening? The parent roles are more than prop roles, since young people tend to handle a problem the way they have seen their parents handle it. This is the Parent Ego State of the P A C concept of Berne and Harris explained above (p. 99). Unless they use new knowledge and experiences to alter it, young people will simply repeat this way of doing things, and pass it on to their children in turn.

Discussion Following the Roleplay. At the end of the roleplay allow each player to express how he is feeling. If two casts are used, compare one with the other. If the boy-player takes the blame for the liquor does he help or hinder the conflict between the parents? Discuss the complications of a third party's presence in the conflict. Does it help or hinder? What actions of the boy-player helped the situation most? Which of his actions were of least value? Did the boy-player get the idea that *he* was the cause of the parents' quarreling? Discuss this feeling and why it is normal for children to feel that way.

Were the parents able to get the liquor problem brought out into the open? Was the question of the wife's working settled? While handling their own problem, how are the parent-players treating the boy? Discuss marriage and the need of support from a marriage partner.

116

NEIGHBORS

Roleplay 17

*Neighbor: Miss Teresa Lambert is an elderly lady who never married. It is hard for her to get along with her next-door neighbors. The children there have very bad manners—they've stomped on her flowers, ruined her trees with climbing, and are now even chasing her cat, Mickie. They keep putting their caged parakeet out on the backyard picnic table even though she had warned them. If Mickie knocked it over and gobbled up the parakeet, there would be the dickens to pay. At the risk of being called a fussy old maid, she is determined to have it out with them.

Mother: Gay has tried to get along with her neighbors, but the elderly woman next door is impossible. The old spinster just doesn't understand children or their needs. She also has a very odd way of looking at problems only from her own point of view. Like the time she wanted them to move their plants because the embankment she had put up so poorly might fall down and crush them. Gay felt that was Teresa's problem not hers, but Roy, her husband, had insisted she move them. Gay is still burned up about that!

Father: Roy can't understand why his wife and children aren't getting along with the sweet little old lady next door. It is about time his children learned a little more consideration for the elderly! As father and head of the household, he's going to see this is corrected. Perhaps he should also insist that his wife show a little more tact.

Anita: Anita, who is eight years old, hates the old hag next door who is so fussy about everything. And Miss Lambert's cat, "dear little Mickie," has been using Anita's sandbox as a toilet! Isn't there a law of some kind that's supposed to keep animals out of other people's yards? The old bag sure seems to think there's a law to keep children out of her yard!

Karl: Karl is a thirteen-year-old boy who tries to get along with the elderly woman next door. But the old witch sure gives him a pain! What did she *expect* him to do when his ball fell into her old flower bed? And her precious trees! Climbing on them doesn't hurt them!

Karen: Karen, who is sixteen, doesn't like the lady next door. Are her parents going to insist she keep her parakeet inside because of the crabby old maid's cat? Dad is unreasonable where this neighbor is concerned. He made her and

*Role-descriptions and dialogue are for conductor only.

her mother move their plants to a new location when it was obvious that the dirt embankment Miss Lambert had put up wouldn't hold. The ole biddy just had to suggest it—and Dad agreed. He should have forced her to put up a proper embankment or replace anything it ruined!

[Father is just leaving for work and the whole family is out in the yard. Miss Lambert sees that they are all together and comes out to talk to them.]

Teresa: I thought you would like to know one of your children has left the parakeet sitting out on the picnic table again.

Karen: Mom, you know my parakeet will just die of a broken heart if he isn't allowed outside!

Mother: It's in a cage, Miss Lambert. Perhaps we can just leave it out and watch it very carefully.

Teresa: Then I suppose you will *all* be chasing Mickie, as your little daughter has been.

Father: Anita, I'm surprised at you. You know better than that!

Anita: But Dad, he uses my sandbox as a toilet!

Father: Anita! Did you hear me? No excuses!

Suggestions for the Roleplay "Neighbors"

Selecting Your Players. Players of any fighting ability can be used with this role. This is a group role, so a player who needs experience in how and when to break into a conversation would be given a chance to try out different ways.

Instructing Your Players. Give each player some psychological help to fight for his particular view. Inform the father-player that he will be playing a rigid prop role, called an assignment role. He will side with the neighbor in everything, and show a complete lack of sympathy for his own family. He will be playing the authoritarian role of the prejudiced parent of the P A C concept (explained in the PAC pinball game, page 99). He will hold rigidly to these instructions throughout the playing. Give him a little help psychologically with something like: "You're ashamed of the way your family is reacting to the elderly neighbor next door. Do your children need a little discipline to behave with respect toward her? And your wife is no help. You'd think she'd have the common decency to show a little tact." Etc. And to bring him into the feel of the scene: "Here comes the sweet little old lady now. How can you help her to feel your sympathy?"

To Gay, the mother, you could say: "You wonder if the elderly woman next door will ever understand your children. Or anyone else's problems but her own! Like that time Roy made you move your plants because she was building an embankment that might fall down. She should have been told that if the embankment did fall *she* would have to have them replanted. You still burn when you think about that!" And to bring her into the scene: "Here she comes now with some new complaint. May the Lord give you patience!"

To Teresa, the neighbor you could say: "You've taken about as much as you can from your neighbor's children." Etc. And to bring her into the scene: "The whole family is out in the yard now. It would be a perfect time to approach them, especially since the parakeet is out on the picnic table again. You put down your broom and go over to talk to them."

The children: To *Karen* you could say: "You wish they had to have cats on a leash when they got out of their own yards. Your neighbor acts like she owns your yard too." Etc. To bring her into the scene: "Here comes the old crab now with something on her mind." Etc. To *Karl* you could say: "The old bag next door sure gave you a bad time about her flowers and trees." Etc. To make him feel a part of the scene: "Here she comes now and you thought she hadn't seen you rescue that ball." To *Anita* you could say: "That stupid cat, 'dear little Mickie,' is ruining your sandbox using it as a toilet. Next time you catch it in your sandbox, you're going to do more than just chase it!" And to bring her into the scene: "Oh boy, here she comes now. You're going to let her know she has to keep her cat in her *own* yard. She expects you to stay out of her yard, doesn't she?"

What to Watch for. How are the other members of the family taking the role of the father-player? Are they hurt by his lack of sympathy? How do they handle this? Does the father-player's action inhibit anyone from taking part in the roleplay? Does the authoritarianism and lack of sympahty from the father bring out the protective feeling in the mother-player? Or does the mother-player feel she must back up the father-player? Do the players believe in their roles or is their body language expressing something different? Are the players leveling about the facts of their roles and about their own feelings? Watch for put-downs and manipulations. Watch for sensitive listening or some form of active listening.

Discussion Following the Roleplay. Reveal that the father was a prop player, and then give each player in turn a chance to tell his reaction to the father's authoritarianism and lack of sympathy. If the mother-player has been protective to counteract the lack of sympathy in the father, can she tell *why* she reacted as she did? If, instead, she backed up her husband, did she do it because "she thought she should"? If she did this, was it clear to the others how she really felt? Discuss this concept, remembering that Gordon in his book *P.E.T.* believes both parents should give their honest reaction rather than agree. Did any of the players try to manipulate? If so, discuss the reaction of the player opposing him. Was it hard for him to fight the manipulation?

119

FUZZY BASEBALL

Game 7

Origin of the word "Fuzzy." The word is taken from a modern fairy tale by Claude Steiner.[2] Briefly, it runs something like this:

"Once upon a time there lived a couple with two children. They were very happy because in those days the good fairy gave everyone at birth a small, soft, Fuzzy Bag containing a supply of Fuzzies that made people feel warm and fuzzy all over. People who didn't get them would develop a sickness and shrivel up and die. Of course they were given freely and very much in demand.

"But the wicked fairy was jealous and she devised a plan to stop this. She told the man that his wife was giving away all of her Fuzzies and soon would not have any left for him. He was very alarmed so he pressured his wife into giving out her Fuzzies more discriminately. The children noticed this and they became stingy. Stinginess spread like wildfire and soon some people were dying.

"The wicked fairy was not interested in having people die, so she gave them a bag with Cold Pricklies that made people feel cold and prickly but prevented them from dying. People began trying to work to earn Fuzzies, but somehow these weren't the same as ones freely given. One entrepreneur even invented the all-purpose Plastic Fuzzy which was supposed to make you feel good but didn't.

"Then a hip woman born under the sign of Aquarius came to the unhappy land, and not knowing about the wicked fairy, again passed out warm Fuzzies to the children. The children loved her and the Fuzzies. They began to give them out freely even though the grownups passed laws against it. What happened then? The outcome is still undecided."

AIM OF THE GAME: To practice giving Fuzzies and get over inhibitions against touching people.

> The game challenges players to see the good points in their fellow players. Implies Fuzzies are important.
>
> (This is a game to be played with a light touch.)

PLAYERS: Five to nine players who form a circle.

> Conductor will act as Umpire and should be generous in calling the hits: the purpose is to stimulate not judge.

Play Action of the Game:

The player at bat goes to each youth in the circle, giving each one a Fuzzy and touching him or her in some way. Players win bases and bring home players as in baseball. Greeting all the players (or 3 outs) completes the game for each. Player with the highest score wins.

Terminology and Rules for Fuzzies:

What is a Fuzzy?—A Fuzzy is more than a compliment. It does not attempt to evaluate the character of a person, but describes that person's efforts, accomplishments, and the warm, friendly, positive feelings he or she engenders in the sender. For a stranger it might be just something nice you have observed. A Fuzzy is not flattery, it must have some basis of truth.

One-Base Hit—A barely passable Fuzzy. Given only when it is obvious the player is not trying very hard.

Two-Base Hit—Good Fuzzy or good gesture. Good for two bases.

Three-Base Hit—A very good Fuzzy or a very good gesture. If both Fuzzy and gesture are very good, it's a home run.

Home Run—An excellent Fuzzy delivered in a smooth way so as not to make a shy person embarrassed. Or, an excellent or original gesture.
Home run brings in all runners on bases.

Strikeout—Called only if player will not even try.

Caught Fly Ball—If the receiver feels the Fuzzy is flattery, he (or she) can declare it false.
If the Umpire agrees he will declare it a fly ball that was caught and call batter out.
If the Umpire does not agree he will call it an error.

Error—Some people find it hard to accept the truth or legitimate Fuzzies. If the receiver declares false something the Umpire feels is a Fuzzy, he can call the receiver on it, getting the support of the other players.
The Umpire will then declare it an error and the player issuing the Fuzzy will get his hit credited.

Foul Ball—Foul ball is called only if the player is constantly using flattery.
If the Umpire feels a Fuzzy is flattery but the recipient says nothing (Umpire must be sure of this), he can say it looks as if the recipient is a little uneasy.
The Umpire will then declare the Fuzzy borderline or a foul ball and the batter will be given another try.

Terminology and Rules for Gestures (Where different):

Gestures—These can be made in a variety of ways and will depend somewhat on how well the sender knows the receiver and how they feel about each other. It can be a kiss, a vigorous hug, a grasping or a touch or pat on the shoulder, a handshake while looking directly at the person and showing some interest, a shove or a jab, or even a gentle fist to a jaw. The more original the better. (Gestures are judged along with the Fuzzies.)

Caught Fly Ball—If the receiver feels the gesture of the batter was not justified, she can object and call it false. Examples:
  a. A youth who is going with a girl may take her in his arms and give her a gentle and lingering kiss. It may be worth a home run.
  b. But if a stranger (or a boy who is aware that the girl does not like him) takes advantage of the opportunity to act in the same way, the girl can object.

If the Umpire feels the girl is justified, he will call it a caught fly ball and declare the batter out.

If he does not agree he will call it an error.

Error—Some people have grown up without showing or receiving physical affection or touching and may object to any gesture. If a receiver calls a gesture false but the Umpire decides it was genuine, he may declare it an error and the batter will get his man on base.

Foul Ball—If a lightweight player shakes hands in a cold or uninterested way, the gesture could be called a foul ball and the batter encouraged to try again. (Conductor should use this sparingly and only when he can help the player.)

If a player keeps giving only handshakes, he can be warned to try something different by calling a foul on him. If he continues, call it bunting.

Bunting—Gestures that are too much the same. They will put a man on base, but not allow the player on third to get home.

Examples of Fuzzies:
1. "My day is brightened by your cheerful smile."
2. "I envy the way you put words together."
3. "I'm put at ease by your friendly manner."
4. "I like the way your eyes sparkle with interest when I am talking with you."
5. "I enjoy talking with you—you seem to listen with your whole being."
6. "Although I don't know you well, I feel you have confidence in yourself by the way you walk and talk."

FARMER-IN-THE-DELL

Game 8

AIM: To learn to give out friendliness, sympathy, and empathy. To allow others to release hidden resentments or emotion.

PLAYERS: Ten to twelve players who form a circle.

TUNE: Game is played to the tune of "The Farmer in the Dell." ("The farmer in the dell, the farmer in the dell, hi ho the dairy oh, the farmer in the dell.")

Play Action:

Farmer: While the group sings the first stanza of "The Farmer in the Dell," the conductor picks a Farmer to start the game.

The conductor explains that Mr. Dell is a stranger in the community and lonely. He needs the friendliness of his neighbors. As Mr. Dell goes around the circle, each person will say a few words in a friendly way to help him feel at ease.

Wife: While the group sings the second stanza of the song, "The farmer takes a wife," Mr. Dell chooses a wife from the circle.

The conductor explains that instead of choosing a Wife from his new neighborhood, as some of the mothers had hoped, Mr. Dell came back from a trip with his new Wife, who is a divorcee and black. (This is an all-white community.) As Mr. Dell takes his Wife around the circle, each one of his neighbors will say something to help her feel she is one of the group.

Child: Mr. Dell goes back into the circle. As the group sings the third stanza of the song, "The wife takes a child," the Wife will choose a Child from the circle.

The conductor explains that this is a Child from the former marriage of the Wife. Some time ago, the Child was hurt in an accident and has lost the use of his (or her) arms.

The doctors feel it is psychosomatic and the Child just needs a great deal of love.

The Wife will take her Child to each of her neighbors and they will say something, or use a gesture of some kind, that will make the Child feel loved.

Dog: The Wife goes back into the circle. As the group sings the fourth stanza, "The child takes a dog," the Child chooses a player from the circle to be the Dog.

The conductor explains that the Dog is feeling low and depressed. He gets only orders barked at him and no love. He feels unloved and unneeded in a cruel world. The Child will take his Dog to each one in the circle and they will try to cheer him up, make him feel wanted and needed, and show him their love.

Cat: The Child goes back into the circle. While the group sings the fifth stanza, "The dog takes a cat," the Dog chooses a Cat from the circle.

The conductor explains that although all of the characters are essentially prop players to stimulate the reaction of the others in the circle, the next three will be playing nasty characters that make if difficult for the rest to respond. (The conductor may prefer to ask for volunteers from here on, or select someone he knows needs to release resentment or emotion.)

The conductor explains that the Cat is playing the part of a person who has been deeply hurt many times and has learned to have little trust and respect for other people. She (he) makes sarcastic and "catty" remarks. (Player may be helped by picturing a cat with an arched back who spits and scratches when anyone gets near.)

The Dog will take the Cat around the group. No matter what the Cat says to them, the players will not get angry and will always act in a positive and loving way.

Rat: The Dog goes back into the circle. While the group sings the sixth stanza, "The cat takes a rat," the Cat will choose a Rat.

The conductor explains that the Rat is playing the part of a person so deeply hurt that he seems to hate everyone around him. He is, however, reacting to the way he has been treated. He is desperately in need of love, but has learned not to show it by acting in a mean and nasty way.

The Cat will take the Rat around the circle and the players will give back loving words for the Rat's nasty remarks. Gestures may also be used. It's to be hoped the Rat will find it harder and harder to play his part.

Cheese: The Cat goes back into the circle. While the group sings the last stanza of the song, "The cheese stands alone," the Rat will choose a Cheese and then go back into the circle.

The conductor explains that the Cheese plays the part of a person who acts like the big cheese. The know-it-all, the person who thinks he should be leading everything. He is obnoxious in his sense of superiority, riding over other people's comments.

The Cheese will go around the circle by himself—he, of course, doesn't feel he needs any help! Each player will try to tell the cheese what they feel he is doing, but in a loving way. They will say things that will show their love and concern while they are telling him they would like to see him change.

Listing as a Discussion Technique: What Is Love?

After any of the roleplays in this chapter, your teenagers may want to discuss love further. Listing the ideas they have about love will help. Ask them for qualities or definitions of love, and for different kinds. Accept all answers your teenagers give, encouraging them to level about their feelings. (The answers below were given by teenagers.[3] They are merely to stimulate your thinking; do not give them unless absolutely necessary.)

1. Love is a sense of understanding, and of being understood.
2. Love is a relationship in which an individual can say what he feels and know the other person goes right on caring about him.
3. Love is a sense of closeness, of belongingness.
4. Love sees the best in another person, but recognizes the everyday side of him.
5. Love is feeling pain when another person is hurt, or anger when he has been treated unfairly.
6. Love is a feeling of happiness so deep that the person in love wants to make everyone else happy, too.
7. Love is wanting the best possible for the other person.
8. Love expresses itself by making an individual want to be the best kind of person he can be, for the sake of the other.

What Are Different Kinds of Love?
1. Mating love—two people facing life's problems together.
2. Physical love or sexual love.
3. Mother love—a nurturing type of love that gives of itself and protects.
4. Possessive love—a smothering type of love that will not allow another person to be himself.
5. Agape love—love of all God's creatures.

For additional reading, see:
George R. Bach and Peter Wyden, *The Intimate Enemy* (New York: Avon Books, 1970).

conclurion

The time in life known as the teenage is filled with a raft of problems. Yet, oddly enough, it is also a time of almost unlimited possibilities. Youths are very susceptible and impressionable, open to idealism and to the setting of idealistic goals. They reach out (sometimes in a halting or clumsy way) for maturity and adulthood. What an opportunity to lend a helping hand!

I hope this book will help your teenagers, and you, to communicate more effectively. Listening, understanding, building a strong self-image, finding out how to deal with courtship and friendship situations—these are all essential to full communication and growth. I sincerely believe that roleplaying is one of the best ways to learn. It brings out communication problems in a way that the players will never forget, and it will help them for a long time to come because of the experiences they'll have of working out difficulties. Although you can use these roleplays over and over, as you become more adept you may want to produce new roles, using the ones here as a basis and bringing in your own counseling experiences. Or you may want to seek out other sources of roleplay to vary the ones here. If the demand is great enough, there might be a sequel to this book with more roleplays.

Gather together about twenty youths. Take them anywhere—to an isolated cabin in the woods or to a cozy room in a church. It won't matter where you are, for once the roleplaying is started, the world outside fades away. You are dealing with in-depth relationships and nothing is more fascinating or more productive of growth. Good luck!

notes

Chapter 2: Instructions

1. I gained my knowledge of roleplaying techniques in Robert Blees' Training Workshops. You may obtain information on these workshops by writing:

> Robert A. Blees
> 2255 Greenville Drive
> West Covina, California 91790.

2. George R. Bach and Peter Wyden, *The Intimate Enemy* (New York: Avon Books, 1970), p. 80.

3. *Ibid.*, p. 324.

4. "We speak at . . . about 125 words per minute . . . . We can think at the rate of 400 to 500 words per minute." From a pamphlet by Robert Haakenson, "The Art of Listening" (Philadelphia: Smith, Kline & French Laboratories, Speakers Bureau & Speech Training Service).

5. From *Are You Listening?* by Ralph G. Nichols and Leonard A. Stevens. Copyright 1957 by McGraw-Hill Book Company. Used with permission of McGraw-Hill Book Company. From pp. 134-137.

6. Thomas Gordon, *P. E. T., Parent Effectiveness Training* (New York: Peter H. Wyden, Inc., 1970), pp. 115-138.

7. *Ibid.*, pp. 121-129.

8. *Ibid.*, p. 63.

Chapter 3: Listening

1. Gordon, *P. E. T.*, pp. 49-61.

2. Copyright © 1970 by Dr. Thomas Gordon. From the book PARENT EFFEC-TIVENESS TRAINING, published by Peter H. Wyden, a division of David McKay Co., Inc. Reprinted & paraphrased with the permission of the publisher. From pp. 41-44.

3. Nichols and Stevens, *Are You Listening?*, chapter 9.

4. *Ibid.*, chapter 11. See p. 18 of the present book.

5. Haim G. Ginott, *Between Parent and Teenager* (New York: The Macmillan Co., 1969), p. 55.

Chapter 4: Understanding

1. Paul Tournier, *To Understand Each Other* (Richmond: John Knox Press, 1967), p. 28.

2. Edward Strecker and Kenneth E. Appel, *Discovering Ourselves* (New York: The Macmillan Co., 1962), pp. 155-161.

3. Frieda Fordham, *An Introduction to Jung's Psychology* (Baltimore: Penguin Books, 1966), pp. 29, 33.

4. Strecker and Appel, *Discovering Ourselves*, pp. 161-169.

5. Tournier, *To Understand Each Other*, p. 31.

6. Maria F. Mahoney, *The Meaning in Dreams and Dreaming* (New York: Citadel Press, 1966), pp. 91-93.

7. *Ibid.*, pp. 93-95.

8. *Ibid.*, p. 89.

9. Fordham, *Introduction to Jung*, pp. 36-38; P. W. Martin, *Experiment in Depth* (New York: Pantheon Books, 1955), p. 22.

10. Fordham, *Introduction to Jung*, p. 42.

11. Jolande Jacobi, *The Psychology of C. G. Jung* (New Haven: Yale University Press, 1962), p. 12.

12. Wheel from *The Psychology of C. G. Jung* by Jolande Jacobi, p. 16. Copyright 1962 by Yale University Press. Used by permission. Sources for adaptation: Martin, *Experiment in Depth*, pp. 22-28; Fordham, *Introduction to Jung*, pp. 36-44.

13. Everett L. Shostrom, *Man, the Manipulator* (Nashville: Abingdon Press, 1967), p. 220. Shostrom says that "one becomes actualizing at that moment when he fully surrenders to the awareness of his manipulations" (p. 222). He believes this occurs in three stages:

    1) Figure out the ways you manipulate and the reason you do.

    2) Restore inner balance by:

        a) Exaggerating manipulative tendencies to experience the foolishness of them.

        b) Expressing the opposite polarity of this pattern.

    3) Put both poles into a unified whole (pp. 218-220).

14. *Ibid.*, pp. 33, 52.

15. *Ibid.*, pp. 36-39.

16. *Ibid.*, figures 1 and 2 on pages 37 and 55. Used by permission.

17. *Ibid.*, pp. 50-51.

Chapter 5: Search for Identity

1. Carl G. Jung, Marie-Louise von Franz, Joseph L. Henderson, Jolande Jacobi, and Aniela Jaffé, *Man and his Symbols* (New York: Dell Publishing Co., 1968), pp. 103-107.

2. Changing the sex of the name can sometimes be accomplished by just adding a feminine or masculine ending. (Feminine endings: a, ia, i, ie, e, ne, ine, isa, itta, itte, ette, it, ica, ika, itsa, iki, anne, illa, alee. Masculine endings: s, as, us, ston, ton, ten, nett, sin, son, ald, dy, le, ley, and, ick, win, ris, ren.) Respelling sometimes involves dropping silent letters (Nicholas, Nichole) and end letters like "w" or "y" (Andrew, Andrea), or changing one letter to another like "y" to "i" or "k" to "c" (Anthony, Antonia). If it becomes necessary to create a new name for a special purpose not mentioned, you can create the name like an *anagram*, switching the letters of a special word or group of words until it has a pleasant sound; *telescoping* by dropping letters from a group of words until you arrive at a suitable name; or *inversion* by switching syllables. From Sue Browder *The New Age Baby Name Book* (New York: Workman Publishing Co., 1974), pp. 16-19.

3. Muriel James and Dorothy Jongeward, *Born to Win* (Reading, Mass.: Addison-Wesley Publishing Co., 1971), pp. 101, 108.

4. Eric Berne, *The Structure and Dynamics of Organizations and Groups* (Philadelphia: J. B. Lippincott, 1963), p. 137.

5. James and Jongeward, *Born to Win*, pp. 127, 128.

6. *Ibid.*, pp. 254-256.

7. *Ibid.*, p. 256.

8. Ann Landers, "Maturity: It Can Mean Many Things," *Wisconsin State Journal* (December 31, 1974), section 2, page 2. Copyright 1974 by Field Newspaper Syndicate. Used by permission.

Chapter 6: The Love-Marriage-Divorce Syndrome

1. Mahoney, *Meaning in Dreams*, pp. 125, 127, 131.

2. Claude Steiner, *Scripts People Live* (New York: Bantam Books, 1975), p. 127. Copyright©1974 by Grove Press. Used by permission.

3. From the book COUNSELING WITH TEENAGERS by Robert Blees. © 1965 by Prentice-Hall, Inc. Published by Prentice-Hall, Inc., Englewood Cliffs, New Jersey. The excerpt is from the Fortress Press reprint (Philadelphia, 1968), p. 115.

8777